Developing Successful Sport Sponsorship Plans

Titles in the Sport Management Library

Developing Successful Sport Sponsorship Plans

— FOURTH EDITION —

David K. Stotlar, EdD
University of Northern Colorado

FiT

Fitness Information Technology

A Division of the International Center
for Performance Excellence
West Virginia University
262 Coliseum, WVU-CPASS
PO Box 6116
Morgantown, WV 26506-6116

Library of Congress Card Catalog Number: 2013940619

ISBN: 978-1-935412-56-4
Cover Design: Bellerophon Productions
Cover Photo: © Banderas/Wikimedia Commons
Typesetter: Bellerophon Productions
Production Editor: Matt Brann
Copyeditor: Geoff Fuller
Proofreader: Rachel Tibbs
Indexer: Rachel Tibbs
Printed by Sheridan Books, Inc.

10 9 8 7 6 5 4 3 2 1

Fitness Information Technology
A Division of the International Center for Performance Excellence
West Virginia University
262 Coliseum, WVU-CPASS
PO Box 6116
Morgantown, WV 26506-6116
800.477.4348 (toll free)
304.293.6888 (phone)
304.293.6658 (fax)
Email: fitcustomerservice@mail.wvu.edu
Website: www.fitinfotech.com

Contents

Detailed Contents

Preface

The fourth edition of *Developing Successful Sport Sponsorship Plans* was developed as a companion to *Fundamentals of Sport Marketing, 4th Edition* (Pitts & Stotlar, 2013). This workbook evolved through several years of developing, reviewing, and critiquing sport sponsorships and draws on the author's experience in academia and the sport industry. While some discussion of sport sponsorship theory is presented in *Fundamentals of Sport Marketing*, this workbook examines the topic from the perspective of the sponsored property, rather than as a marketing tactic. It provides an overview of the theoretical underpinnings of the topic, followed by examples from actual sport sponsorships. In some cases, the name of the sport organization has been changed for reasons of confidentiality. Most chapters provide worksheets for use in constructing quality sponsorship proposals. The intent of this book is simple: to provide a workbook that assists individuals in creating a sponsorship proposal through well-defined, industry-proven protocol. A sequential process is provided to build a quality sponsorship proposal that ensures success. Enjoy the workbook and good luck in seeking sport sponsorships.

Acknowledgments

I first want to recognize the support and understanding of my wife and life partner, Sylvia. Without her sense of humor and challenges to my naïve comments, the book would be less interesting. I also want to thank all the students and colleagues who, over the years, have been willing to tell me exactly what they think about the book. Many students working in industry often call and say they are using what they learned and have kept the books as a guide. This is the ultimate compliment—that the material is usable and pertinent to success in the industry.

I also want to thank the publisher and editors at Fitness Information Technology for their patience and persistence in the development and publication of this edition. I look forward to many future editions.

—David K. Stotlar

1

Understanding Sport Sponsorship

INTRODUCTION

Sponsorship, in its essence, is based on a mutual exchange between a sport entity and a corporation (Copeland, Frisby, & McCarville, 1996; McCarville & Copeland, 1994). This reliance on exchange theory suggests that both entities can simultaneously provide and receive benefits. Thus, a symbiotic relationship can be attained. In the case of adidas's sponsorship of the New Zealand All Blacks rugby team, Motion, Leitch, and Brodie (2003, p. 1083) noted that "in sponsorship both the sponsor and the sponsored activity become involved in a symbiotic relationship with a transference of inherent values from the activity to the sponsor." In the United States and many other nations, sport organizations have aggressively marketed themselves to sponsors in an effort to obtain the funds necessary to operate programs. Seaver's research with 50 of the top U.S. sponsors indicated that 10% of sponsoring companies get more than 1300 proposals per year (Seaver, 2004). North American 2012 sponsorship spending was projected to reach $18.9 billion, up 4.1% over 2011 ("2013 Sponsorship Outlook," 2013).

The major areas of the economy where sponsorship spending is apportioned remained constant over the last few years and have been noted below (www.sponsorship .com/Resources/Sponsorship-Spending.aspx):

Sports: 69%

Entertainment: 10%

Cause Marketing: 9%

Arts: 5%

Festivals/Fairs: 4%

Associations and Member Organizations: 3%

Financial expenditures on sponsorship activities were not limited to North America. Total global spending for 2012 was projected at $51 billion (www.sponsorship.com/Re sources/Sponsorship-Spending.aspx), with projections for a 13% growth through 2015 (pwc.com/sportsoutlook). International corporate spending also escalated in 2012 as

European corporations contributed $14.1 billion in sponsorship deals. Much of the European spending resulted from sponsorships surrounding the 2012 Olympic Games. Sponsorships across soccer in Europe remained relatively flat (www.sponsorship.com/Resources/Sponsorship-Spending.aspx).

Pacific Rim countries accounted for $11.9 billion, and Central and South America spent an additional $5.4 billion. Various other regional spending accounted for $2.2 billion, bringing the worldwide 2012 total to $451 billion. With an increase of 14.8% above 2007 revenues, it seems sponsorship presents an opportunity for the growing list of multinational companies (www.sponsorship.com/Resources/Sponsorship-Spending.aspx).

There is an increasing need for sport administrators and managers to understand the methodologies of this marketing component. Sponsorship has been defined as "a cash and/or in-kind fee paid to a property (typically sports, arts, entertainment, or causes) in return for access to the exploitable commercial potential associated with that property" (Ukman, 2004a, p. 154).

Some concerns exist as to whether the sports sponsorship field is saturated or will continue to grow in the years ahead. There is also an emerging trend toward both convergence and competition between sport and entertainment. This can be seen when the network that secures broadcast rights for a league leverages those rights for cameo appearances of popular athletes. The leagues also suggest product placement in television shows with items like team jerseys or background screens of league games. According to Spanberg (2011) "Each of the major leagues has one, if not several, executives working on vetting and making pitches to be included in shows and movies" (p. 22). This is an exciting but complicated trend. If a player is used in a TV shot wearing his jersey at the team stadium, the process requires negotiations with the player's agent, the league for use of its licensed jersey, and the owner of the stadium. Yes, it's a crazy world we live in.

Another trend noted by Price-Waterhouse-Cooper is that sport managers must develop more sophisticated measures for sponsorship activities ("PwC Outlook," n.d.). Historically, sport properties have pursued and negotiated with sponsors in a singular and direct manner. However, Burton and O'Reilly (2010) forecast that sponsors may be trending toward developing "sponsor alliances" wherein groups of sponsors band together and negotiate collectively with sport properties. Burton and O'Reilly ask, "What if the sponsors from all major North American sports were to form a syndicate?" (p. 21). This would surely constitute a shift in power and propel massive changes across the industry. Just a thought.

Many sports are heavily engaged in sponsorship (e.g., professional football, basketball, tennis and golf) while others are less involved. From high school sports to college programs to professional leagues, everyone seems to want to be involved in sport sponsorship. The potential is so great that the Carroll Independent School District in Texas hired a full-time director of sponsorships. San Antonio opted to hire an agency with the school district, keeping 35% of the revenues ("A Tale of Two Districts," 2003). High schools in Texas and North Carolina went so far as to pursue naming rights for their facilities, a practice once reserved for professional teams. One high school near the Dallas-Fort Worth airport secured $4 million from Dr. Pepper to place a logo on the school's roof to be seen by airline passengers (Popke, 2002). High school state athletic associations are also moving into the sponsorship realm. Revenues for "all sports—all championships" range from a high of about $500,000 (California) to a low of $200,000 (New Mexico). In all, about 24 of the 50 high school athletic associations have some type of sponsorship program (Carey, 2012).

At the collegiate level, about 10% of income for the National Collegiate Athletic Association (NCAA) Division I programs comes from sponsorship revenue with the average sponsorship for an NCAA Division I institution at $1.13 million (Drayer, Shapiro, & Morse, 2012). The trend in major college athletic departments has been to outsource their sponsorship and media rights to agencies. IMG College and Learfield Communications are the leading agencies. IMG College represents almost 100 of the premier institutions and has been actively engaged in packaging portfolios of teams for select sponsors. Similarly, Fishbait Marketing secured the rights for 33 college bowl games through the Football Bowl Association in 2012. This would allow sponsors to negotiate with Fishbait for opportunities across several games. These creative one-stop-shopping scenarios mimic many of the advantages of the International Olympic Committee's TOP program. The NCAA granted exclusive marketing rights to Turner Sports and CBS Sports, who run their Corporate Champions and Corporate Partners program.

Professional sport leagues have been able to increase sponsorship revenues substantially over the years. Control over the league's sponsorship is continually a topic in owners' meetings. Many owners want to preserve marketing rights for the team while others, principally in small-market cities, advocate league-wide sponsorships where revenues are shared equally across all teams.

In an effort to minimize the overabundance of signage inside sport stadiums, some professional teams (e.g., Florida Marlins with the 2012 Marlins Park) began to segment their stadiums. This concept involved the development of sponsor zones, each dedicated to a single sponsor extending from banners on parking lot light poles to entrances and culminating with field, court, and scoreboard signage inside the facility. Similarly, the MetLife Stadium in New Jersey and the Daytona International Speedway opted for branded entrances as additions for 2012/2013.

Park and recreation departments are also engaged in sport sponsorship activities. Beyond the longstanding traditions of sponsors for Little League teams and outfield signage at the ballpark, some park and recreation mangers are exploring new ground. For example, Gatorade signed a deal with Virginia Beach Parks and Recreation Department in which Gatorade did not pay an upfront fee but based their fee on product sales. They provided $6,000 for the first 1,600 cases of Gatorade sold, $3,000 for the next 1,600, and $1,000 for every additional 1,600 cases sold. The entire sponsorship fee amounted to $15,000 over three years.

What initially attracted sponsors to sport is the ability to reach consumers in a less cluttered environment than traditional advertising (Pitts & Stotlar, 2013; Skildum-

Reid, 2012). The clutter in advertising is such that the average consumer is exposed to over 5,000 messages every day. Sponsorship had the potential to deliver advertising messages more effectively than established advertising channels. However, sport may now have become oversaturated. According to Skildum-Reid (2012), many sport events have become cluttered with title sponsors, presenting sponsors, supporting sponsors, cam-sponsors, official product sponsors, pouring rights, and licensing rights. Clutter and dilution are in direct opposition to what sponsors want. She also noted that the clutter and overabundance of signage is atrocious. What sponsorship intends to do is "connect with people through something they care about" (Skildum-Reid, 2012, p. 3).

As an example of the clutter issue, Spanberg (2012a) noted that fans at a NASCAR race are exposed to 2,000 brand images compared to about 200 at the average MLB game. Clutter interrupts rather than enhances the audience's experience with the event. In a cluttered market, many sponsors are seeking alternatives to mainstream sport, moving instead to action or extreme sports. Not only have they found these markets less cluttered, but the events have a strong psychographic pull with 18–24-year-old consumers (Cordiner, 2002).

Several authorities note sponsors are changing their strategy for sponsorship. The emerging theme is fewer, bigger, better. Poole (2003, p. 14) said that sponsors "would rather spend more money on bigger properties than spread their sponsorships around to more numerous, smaller properties." In 2010, the University of Michigan moved to a "less is more" stance for their sponsorship. Their goal was to reduce clutter and provide better service to their marketing partners by decreasing the total number of sponsors. A similar trend was seen at the World Cup in soccer where the number of sponsors was reduced to 28—15 partners plus official suppliers and licensees. Seaver's corporate survey revealed the same trend. One executive commented, "We are doing fewer programs in the coming year; however, the programs that we're staying with will be bigger and better" (Seaver, 2004, p. 19). Another said, "What we'll be doing, we'll be doing at a higher level. Big impact is better for us, we feel, than a lot of small sponsorships. This will affect the second-tier sports and the number of people we will be talking to" (p. 20).

The issue of clutter also affects the methods with which sponsors choose to communicate with consumers. Researchers at an event in Holland found that some sponsors were labeled "uncool" because their presence was too obvious, while sponsors that had relevant activation were perceived more favorably. According to Ukman (2003a, p. 2), "There is a huge gap between how marketers want to reach people and how people want to be reached." Similarly, Dan Migala, author of the industry insider newsletter "The Migala Report," noted that sponsorships are most effective when they enhance the participant's experience rather than detract from it. Visiting with participants in the New York City Marathon, Dan found that they particularly liked the activation by Gatorade and Dunkin' Donuts who provided refreshments during the event. UPS also enhanced the runners' experiences by having its Big Brown trucks deliver runners' personal belongings from the starting area to the finish line (Migala, 2007b). Thoughtfully designed sponsorships can bridge the gap between interruption and enhancement.

SPONSORSHIP BACKGROUND

In the early history of sport marketing, sponsorship activities often served the interests of corporate CEOs—as if they were saying, for example, "Let's sponsor golf, because I like golf." This allowed company executives to mix socially with elite athletes and also to provide client entertainment activities. However, these rationales have almost disappeared in the modern era of sport sponsorship. Nevertheless, most major sporting events continue to provide hospitality areas as part of sponsorship packages where executives can meet with celebrity-athletes before and after the competition. Notwithstanding these possibilities, greater sophistication evolved after the 1980s and 1990s, with the introduction of philanthropy to sport sponsorship.

There has been a considerable amount of debate about whether companies engage in sponsorship activities for philanthropic reasons or for financial benefits. Moreover, an interesting new term was recently introduced into the realm of business management. *Strategic philanthropy* has been defined as "a company's long-term investment in an appropriate cause that does measurable good in society while enhancing the company's reputation with key audiences" (Jones, 1997, p. 33). In 2004, IEG began conducting seminars on strategic philanthropy for its corporate clients. The seminars focused on "Leveraging Philanthropy with Marketing" and "Putting Hope and Heart into Sales" ("Strategic Philanthropy," 2004). Social responsibility has been an aspect of corporate philosophy for many years and numerous sport causes have benefited as a result. Corporations have donated to many different programs, and through this corporate giving, they have assisted programs in art, sport, medicine, and culture. However, corporate motives must be examined.

Whether or not a company engages in altruistic philanthropy, research has shown that consumers are influenced by a company's charitable activities. It has been found that 14% of consumers sought out companies with viable corporate philanthropy programs and 40% saw a company's corporate citizenship as a tie-breaker when deciding which company to patronize (Jones, 1997). Research also showed that the overlay of a cause could lead to increased purchase intent if there is little difference between brands on quality and price. However, the positive effects of cause-related marketing appear to diminish as the difference in competing brands increases (Roy & Graeff, 2003). There are many corporations that tie sport and cause-related marketing together. Verizon Wireless sponsors a team of professional women cyclists who volunteer to give any winnings to HopeLine, Verizon's initiative to help victims of domestic violence. They also created a program through HopeLine, and the Miami Heat collected wireless phones, handsets, batteries, and accessories from any carrier at the Verizon Wireless kiosk inside the stadium and refurbished them for victims of domestic violence ("HopeLine Success Stories," n.d.).

While it may seem ludicrous, some corporate officers talk about "owning a cause" (Jones, 1997, p. 36), which sounds more like a marketing strategy than true philanthropy. But, according to Jones (1997, p. 34), "It [doesn't] take long for consumers to see these tactics as sales pitches thinly veiled in the guise of social activism."

Granted, there may be corporations that engage in sport sponsorship for truly philanthropic reasons. However, the record shows that charitable approaches have limited success in securing corporate sponsorships. Corporate self-interest has been considerably more viable as a motivation for involvement with sport sponsorship. (A closer look at the reasons why businesses would be attracted to sport is detailed in Chapter 3.)

Some of the more prominent justifications reveal that sport is attractive to sponsors because it can provide a cross-sectional demographic exposure when compared to other marketing avenues. The diverse demographics represented by many sport activities and events is crucial to corporations, and thus, to the creation of potential sponsorship affiliations.

Sponsoring sport often adds a double exposure for sponsors with on-site promotional activities and media coverage. Typically, when an athlete wins a major tournament or event, their picture shows up on media websites and newspapers across the country. One sport marketer commented that you can buy the back page of *Sports Illustrated*, but you can't buy the front.

On the other hand, not all sponsorship is positive or even intentional. For example, an interesting yachting incident occurred when an America's Cup boat sponsored by Oracle obtained significant exposure for its sponsor by capsizing under the Golden Gate Bridge during the race. The overturned boat was in range of television and news cameras, and it appeared on networks and newspaper front pages worldwide, displaying the sponsor's name. Although it was not the type of publicity that the sponsor had in mind, people around the globe turned their newspapers sideways to read the sponsor's name on the side of the boat.

DEPENDENCE ON SPONSORSHIP

There are some authorities who believe that sport has become overly dependent on corporate sponsors to meet expenses. Two examples show that too much dependence on sponsors could have disastrous effects. In China, an international badminton tournament was canceled when sponsors pulled out during an economic downturn. Also, during the economic difficulties from 2008–2009, the LPGA lost several Title sponsors.

Dependence on sponsorship monies is also evident with colleges and universities that rely on corporations and sponsorship revenues for additional income. The University of Nebraska pooled all of its sponsorship and media assets and signed a 13-year agreement with IMG. Including the sponsorship rights held by the athletic department, the total value of the 13-year package was $143 million (University of Nebraska Board of Regents, 2008). Nike has all-sport agreements with 20 top college programs while adidas has deals with about 15, including Texas A&M University and the University of Michigan, which both switched in 2008 from Nike to adidas. The Texas A&M deal was reportedly worth $60 million in cash and merchandise with a $6.5 million signing bonus. Relative newcomer Under Armour also has a significant group of universities under contract. Many educational institutions have realized the kinds of benefits associated with sponsorship deals:

1. Free equipment
2. Stadium advertising
3. Supplements to coaches' salaries
4. Television revenues for regular and post-season games.

Colleges and universities in the U.S. have realized profits in the millions of dollars from corporate-sponsored football bowl games. The Bowl Championship Series games payout figures have been staggering. For 2013, the per-team payout for the BCS Bowl, Tostitos Fiesta Bowl, FedEx Orange Bowl, Allstate Sugar Bowl, and the Rose Bowl (presented by Visio) were $18 million. With the change in bowl championship structure beginning in the 2013–14 season, the payouts were not determined at press time.

In an attempt to gain greater control over sponsorship, the NCAA, along with many professional sports teams, has imposed rules regarding the size of corporate logos that can be displayed on team uniforms and equipment because of overt commercialization. However, in a lawsuit against the NCAA, apparel companies questioned the NCAA's motives when the bowl game corporate sponsors were allowed to place logos that exceeded the legal size limits on uniforms during the post-season games.

Major League Baseball (MLB) also implemented rules about the size of logos on bats after the All Star Game when a player held his bat up to the camera to display its oversized logo: a promotion ski racers have been known to do at the end of a race as well.

The National Football League (NFL) and the National Hockey League created significant controversy by controlling the display of logos on player apparel. Their regulations state that manufacturers must pay the league a fee for the right to display their marks during a game. Thus, an NFL player who has an endorsement deal (see Chapter 5) cannot display a corporate logo on his shoes if the shoe company has not paid the league a rights fee. To illustrate the height to which this controversy has risen, the NFL fined Chicago Bear player Brian Urlacher $100,000 for wearing a hat with logos of Gatorade's competitor on a team media day. Gatorade is an official sponsor of the NFL.

MLB has not operated without controversy in this area either. MLB owners relinquished their rights to sign exclusive team agreements with uniform shoe manufacturers. Previously, each individual team could sign with a single company (e.g., adidas with the New York Yankees). However, in an out-of-court legal settlement, the uniform rights for all teams now reside with Major League Baseball Properties. In another control-oriented issue, the Baltimore Orioles attempted to stop three players from promoting Pepsi products because the team had an agreement with Coca-Cola. In 2012, the NFL contracts for rising stars Andrew Luck and Robert Griffin III contained clauses that required the player to make "good faith efforts" to work with team sponsors (Mullen, 2012). The question at hand appears to be, Who has the right to control player sponsorships, the player or the League?

CREATING WIN-WIN-WIN STRATEGIES

According to Skildum-Reid (2012) the old win-win (property-sponsor) focus left out the most important aspect of sponsorship, the sponsor's target market. The number one connection in the sponsorship equation is "the connection between the sponsor's brand and the target market" (p. 17). Thus we have win-win-win. This is "the number one concept that drives best practice" (p. 16). Sports activities and corporations can create symbiotic relationships that are greater than the sum of the separate entities. Ukman (2004b, p. 2) reported that "combining the assets of allied organizations creates sponsorship platforms in which the whole is worth more than the sum of the individual parts." Sport managers want to increase their revenues and the exposure of their programs. Coincidentally, sport sponsors want to increase their revenues and the exposure of their products. A sport sponsorship arrangement can fulfill these needs for each organization. Kim Skildum-Reid (2012) goes one step further and recommends a win-win-win protocol that includes not only the sponsors and the organization, but the consumer (participant or spectator) as well. In general, corporations are interested in marketing their products and services to potential customers. If sport can provide a vehicle for this endeavor, then a successful relationship can be established. The task for the sport marketing professional is to make it clear to the sponsor just how this can be accomplished through his or her organization or event. It is also critical that sponsorships enhance the experience of the participants and spectators rather than detract from it.

CONTROVERSIES

Not everyone agrees that involvement with corporate sponsorships is beneficial for sport. Sport marketers should, therefore, be aware that not all members of the community embrace their involvement with certain corporate sponsors. Many feel that blending alcohol and tobacco with the healthful benefits of sports is hypocritical; as a result, there have been several moves on the part of government entities and regulating bodies to restrict alcohol and tobacco advertising in sport settings.

Tobacco and Alcohol Sponsorship

Considerable debate surrounded a European Union ban on tobacco advertising in sport. The French government has had a ban in place for many years and has been pushing the application of legislation throughout Europe. The restrictions on tobacco sponsorship in sport vary across Europe. While a ban in the United Kingdom went into effect in 2006, the German government contended that smoking was a health issue, and therefore, should be within the control of the individual nations. Most of the alcohol and tobacco sponsorship has eroded in Europe although the heavy dependence of Formula One racing on tobacco sponsorship was an exception. This led some organization executives to plan for races at venues in countries more sympathetic to tobacco advertising (Currie, 2004).

The Australian government adopted legislation to restrict tobacco advertising, but the regulations allow events of "international significance" to apply for an exemption. The Canadian government also enacted legislation that restricted the display of tobacco advertising in sport. As of 1998, sport and cultural groups got a five-year reprieve from the government's tough tobacco advertising restrictions (Danylchuk, 1998). Existing signage was allowed to remain through 2000, and from 2000–2003, advertising by tobacco companies was limited to on-site displays and relegated to the bottom 10% of the sign (Danylchuk, 1998).

The French, Canadian, and Australian governments are but a few of those taking action on the issue. There may be many more in waiting, including measures in the United States resulting from a settlement between various states and the tobacco industry that addressed payments for medical coverage for smokers.

In the U.S., the Family Smoking Prevention and Tobacco Control Act (Tobacco Control Act) became law in 2009. It gave the Food and Drug Administration the authority to regulate the manufacture, distribution, and marketing of tobacco. This legislation banned "tobacco product sponsorship of sporting and entertainment events under the brand name of cigarettes or smokeless tobacco" (FDA, 2012, "What the Tobacco . . ." section, para. 2).

The controversy of beer advertising has not been as well publicized as tobacco. Internationally, the laws vary between countries. The NCAA has also restricted alcohol advertising such that beer and wine products (not exceeding 6% alcohol by volume) are allowable, provided such advertisements do not compose more than 14% of the space in the NCAA publication (e.g., game program) devoted to advertising or not more than 60 seconds per hour of any NCAA championship programming, and that such advertisements or advertisers incorporate "Drink Responsibly" educational messaging. Alcohol advertising is not permitted at NCAA Championship events (NCAA, n.d.).

Virtual Signage

Virtual signage has been one of the recent developments that challenge both sport marketers and event owners. With the technology behind virtual signage, "advertisers can insert their logo or brand message on the field in football, behind the batter in baseball, along the glass in hockey and more, all from a remote operation in real-time" (Sportvision, n.d., para. 1). A variety of sport organizations allow for use of this technology while others restrict or prohibit its use. Major League Baseball (MLB) has been the most prolific user, placing virtual ads behind home plate in regular and post-season play. Other sports have also explored the use of this new technology. World Wrestling Entertainment, the X-Games, and various professional tennis tournaments have readily implemented virtual signage. The controversy centers around control of the images that are presented on the field. Many facility owners convinced sponsors to purchase stadium advertising with the idea that these signs would be seen on television. However, with this technology, not only could existing stadium advertising be blocked out, but a competitor's advertising could be inserted via this computer technology.

Another point of contention has been the inclusion of sponsor signage in video games. Electronic Arts (EA), one of the leading producers of video games, has used a marketing theme: "If it's in the game, it's in the game." Up to this point, they have included signage in almost all of their games. Many sport marketers feel that these actions present an excellent opportunity to market to children in an authentic environment. EA

Sports Director of Sports Marketing commented that "video games are a perfect vehicle for companies to target an attentive teenage audience" ("EA Sports," 1998). There are, however, others who believe that this step represents another unconscionable intrusion into society.

In summary, the relationship between sport organizations and sponsors must include advantages for all parties. This win-win-win situation can provide market value and higher profits for corporations, and increase operating revenues for sport organizations and events. An overall view of the sponsorship process is provided in the Best Practice section that follows. The task for a sport marketing professional is to make it clear to the sponsor just how this can be accomplished through a particular sport organization or event.

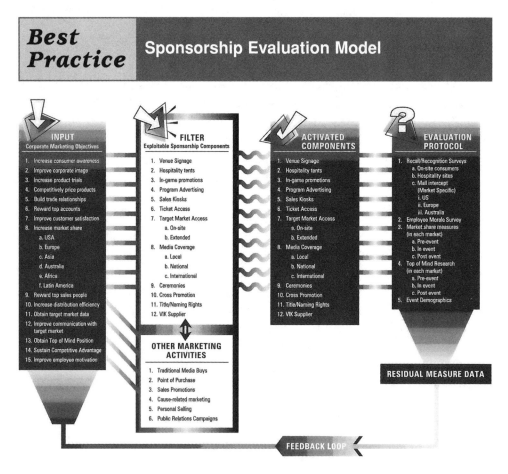

Best Practice — Sponsorship Evaluation Model

INPUT — Corporate Marketing Objectives
1. Increase consumer awareness
2. Improve corporate image
3. Increase product trials
4. Competitively price products
5. Build trade relationships
6. Reward top accounts
7. Improve customer satisfaction
8. Increase market share
   a. USA
   b. Europe
   c. Asia
   d. Australia
   e. Africa
   f. Latin America
9. Reward top sales people
10. Increase distribution efficiency
11. Obtain target market data
12. Improve communication with target market
13. Obtain Top of Mind Position
14. Sustain Competitive Advantage
15. Improve employee motivation

FILTER — Exploitable Sponsorship Components
1. Venue Signage
2. Hospitality tents
3. In-game promotions
4. Program Advertising
5. Sales Kiosks
6. Ticket Access
7. Target Market Access
   a. On-site
   b. Extended
8. Media Coverage
   a. Local
   b. National
   c. International
9. Ceremonies
10. Cross Promotion
11. Title/Naming Rights
12. VIK Supplier

OTHER MARKETING ACTIVITIES
1. Traditional Media Buys
2. Point of Purchase
3. Sales Promotions
4. Cause-related marketing
5. Personal Selling
6. Public Relations Campaigns

ACTIVATED COMPONENTS
1. Venue Signage
2. Hospitality tents
3. In-game promotions
4. Program Advertising
5. Sales Kiosks
6. Ticket Access
7. Target Market Access
   a. On-site
   b. Extended
8. Media Coverage
   a. Local
   b. National
   c. International
9. Ceremonies
10. Cross Promotion
11. Title/Naming Rights
12. VIK Supplier

EVALUATION PROTOCOL
1. Recall/Recognition Surveys
   a. On-site consumers
   b. Hospitality sites
   c. Mall intercept
      (Market Specific)
      i. US
      ii. Europe
      iii. Australia
2. Employee Morale Survey
3. Market share measures
   (in each market)
   a. Pre-event
   b. In event
   c. Post event
4. Top of Mind Research
   (in each market)
   a. Pre-event
   b. In event
   c. Post event
5. Event Demographics

RESIDUAL MEASURE DATA

FEEDBACK LOOP

Sponsorship Worksheets

These worksheets provide a guide to developing various sections of a sponsorship plan. The following sheets cover possible corporate rationale for sponsorship, legal restrictions, and controversies. Complete this worksheet as you would prepare a sponsorship plan.

Determine possible rationale(s) that corporations may have for sponsoring your team, organization, or event.

_____
_____
_____
_____
_____
_____
_____
_____
_____
_____

Discuss any legal restrictions (e.g., tobacco and alcohol laws) that would affect the sponsorship of your team, organization, or event.

_____
_____
_____
_____
_____
_____
_____
_____
_____

Consider any possible controversies that may influence the sponsorship of your team, organization, or event.

_____
_____
_____
_____
_____
_____
_____
_____
_____

2

Prospecting for Sponsors

IDENTIFYING SPONSORS

Involvement with sporting events and sports organizations is not the right partnership for everyone. In an off-handed comment at a national forum on sport sponsorships, one presenter made light of legal troubles incurred at the 2012 Winter Olympic Games by joking that a law firm should become the official legal counsel for the International Figure Skating Federation. Some things don't always fit. On the other hand, 2004 marked the first year that the Super Bowl named an official law firm—Winstead, Sechrest, and Minick, who worked with the Houston organizing committee during the bidding process and even into contract negotiations with the league and vendors.

Not all businesses in a community have the ability or the interest to buy into sport sponsorships, but some companies naturally fit with sport sponsorship. For example, Colorado State University, whose mascot is a Ram, acquired Dodge trucks as a sponsor of their coach's show. Gatorade, developed in 1965 by University of Florida doctors to help re-hydrate their football players, has been a staple on NFL and college sidelines for 45 years. When the television audience sees a Gatorade cooler on the field, they know that the product works. Pepsi, owner of the Gatorade brand, extended its sponsorship with the NFL in 2011.

Sport marketers can find those businesses that have both an interest and the ability to participate. Sponsorship pioneer David Wilkinson said, "Make no mistake. The process of finding sponsors and then showing them how you can help them requires imagination and marketing effort" (1986, p. 40). As a starting point, sport marketers research the current trends within individual business sectors. Articles, trade publications, and industry websites are often great sources of information on corporate activity. Simply reading about local businesses is a convenient place to begin. If you are dealing with the prospect of national sponsorships, the nation's leading business sources, like the Wall Street Journal, are useful resources. Looking for information on corporate mergers, business expansion, and product launches can be profitable. When financial services giant Wachovia merged with Wells Fargo bank in 2008, they embarked on a massive sponsorship campaign across the northeast and secured a variety of sponsorship rights and team deals as a result. Through the merger, the Wachovia Center in Philadelphia became the Wells Fargo Center.

In another example, the Boston Marathon brought in the Mercedes Group for the 2004 race and its launch of the SMART brand. The race offered substantial media exposure and 500,000 on-course spectators. SMART brand executives noted, "SMART drivers have a lot in common with marathon runners. They are more active than average and have a variety of interests. They have a zest for life, a great deal of enthusiasm and do not define themselves by age and social background, but by intellectual and creative potential. The SMART brand will offer products that appeal to this audience in the United States" ("Smart Brand Vehicles," 2004). Noting business activity like this certainly adds to the possibilities of finding sponsors who could benefit from a sport marketing platform.

Access to this type of information also comes through sport sponsorship trade publications. Trade publications in the sport business field, such as *IEG Sponsorship Report* and *SportsBusiness Journal*, are valuable sources of information. *IEG Sponsorship Report* regularly publicizes the most active categories involved in sponsorship, such as nonalcoholic beverages (where 22% of properties had one as a sponsor), banks (19%), automotive products (18%), telecommunications (17%), beer (14%), insurance (12%), and specialty retail (12%) ("IEG Property Survey," 2011). Therefore, companies in these economic sectors may be likely candidates to approach for sponsorship.

The local Chamber of Commerce is also a good source of information for analysis as it typically includes records such as business profiles covering personnel, financial bases, and company products. Other traditional sources suggested by Wilkinson (1986) include looking through the telephone book, examining ads in the newspaper, and simply taking a drive through the business district to stimulate your imagination in an effort to create a potential match. Another technique that has proven successful is examining specific business relations of a sport organization or institution. There may be some natural relationships that would be strengthened through a sponsorship agreement.

Many times businesses that you collaborate with have a vested interest in your success. Perhaps the best example of this concept is the enormously successful sponsorship of Hendrick Motorsport by DuPont. Understanding the circumstances shows that the Hendrick Automotive Group owns more than 100 automotive dealerships, has 7,000 employees and has over $3.5 billion in annual revenues. Each of these dealerships maintains a collision repair facility that purchases a massive amount of automotive paint. DuPont Automotive Finishes happens to be one of the leading retailers of automotive paint. Thus, Hendrick Motorsport gained sponsorship of one of its racecars, driven by Jeff Gordon, and DuPont gained product sales and significant other benefits through the relationship (Hagstrom, 1998; "Rick Hendrick," n.d.).

In a similar move, Glidden Paints entered into a partnership with the Big South Conference as its official paint supplier. "The partnership will allow Glidden Professional Paints the opportunity to claim a strong foothold in a league that spends a large sum on paint and supplies each year" (p. 2). Although not specifically mentioned, the relationship allowed Glidden access to the entire university system of all members of the Big South Conference, which includes students, faculty, and staff who also buy paint (Big South, 2010).

As a follow-up step, the reader should generate a list of businesses and corporations that assess the criteria delineated in Chapter 3. Thereafter, rank the potential for each business listed as a starting place for sponsor prospecting.

Finding the correct point of access is often difficult. Some retail outlets arrange their own sponsorship agreements while, in other situations, sponsorships are administered from corporate headquarters. Many local businesses are affiliated with franchises and chains of similar stores (such as Pizza Hut, McDonalds, and True Value Hardware Stores). In some cases, the marketer may need to go through the corporate headquarters for approval. This is not always a disadvantage as the main corporation may have more money to commit than does a local retailer, and corporate executives may be willing to utilize ideas to promote the entire company. Regardless of where the final decision is made, a sport marketer should always visit with the local franchise owner or distributor first. If a sport marketer attempts to find a sponsor without at least tacit support from a local retailer, chances of success will be diminished. The Coors Beer example in the Best Practice section at the end of this chapter shows how the costs for sponsorship on some ventures were set up on a cooperative, shared-cost basis (also refer to Chapter 8 for more detail on corporate access).

Before asking a corporate sponsor what their business objectives are, research the following questions:

1. What type of product or service does the corporation produce?
2. What is their marketing structure?
3. What are their general marketing approaches?
4. What types of programs are successful?
5. Where does the corporation stand in relation to their competition?
6. Have they used sports and/or events previously, and if so, was their experience positive or negative?
7. Who makes their marketing decisions?

INVESTIGATING POTENTIAL SPONSORS

One of the keys to success is the ability to investigate the sponsoring company. Do the homework! The first step in investigating a corporation is gaining access to their corporate literature, such as their annual report. Begin by looking for the annual report directly from the company website or request it from the corporate office. The Securities and Exchange Commission (SEC) requires all publicly held companies in the U.S. with over 500 shareholders and $10 million in assets to file annual reports. Information in these reports can be accessed through the SEC's website (www.sec.gov) and through the Public Register's Annual Report Service (www.prars.com). These documents will tell you a lot about the inner workings of the target companies. There are, however, many things that a company doesn't want the public and their shareholders to know that the sport marketer needs to know. For example, just knowing who holds what office is not enough: You must know who the power brokers are in the corporation. For this perspective, read clippings from area newspapers or talk to people who do business with the company.

The process also involves a thorough investigation of the sponsor's business structure. Sport marketers cannot possibly convince a sponsor that they are working in a sponsor's best interest without fully comprehending the sponsor's business. The senior marketing manager for Gulf States Toyota said, "The most critical tactic for a property that wants to work with us is to show us that they understand our business. It would go a long way in my eyes to know that a property had talked to dealers and sales people before even talking to me" (Williamson, 2004, p. 5).

A sport marketer's research should also investigate corporate ownership. In today's business world, the complexity of ownership means that companies you may be approaching have strong national and international ties. Pizza Hut, Kentucky Fried Chicken, and Taco Bell were, for many years, owned by PepsiCo (they are now affiliate operations under Yum Brands). Would McDonald's become involved in a sponsorship that also included Pepsi? This would most likely never happen because of the strong ties between Coke and McDonald's through their restaurant association and their Olympic sponsorship alliance. Another specific example was the 2013 renewal of Pepsi with Hendrick Motorsports when team driver Dale Earnhardt Jr.'s pending sponsorship deal with Subway (Coke is Subway's pouring partner) was vetoed by Pepsi. However, Subway is not without its own leverage as Frito-Lay (owned by Pepsi) chips may disappear from Subway racks (Lefton, 2012a).

In many instances, a sport organization's financial partners may also serve as potential sponsors. Most professional sport organizations and many college athletic departments associated themselves with national banking conglomerates to issue Affinity Cards. These credit cards feature team logos, providing increased incentive for their customers to choose a bank's card while benefiting the sport organization or league. Through these partnerships, the sport organization receives a set payment per subscriber and a percentage of sales generated from card use.

As noted earlier, the search for sponsors can be demanding and involves significant hours of research and investigation. However, it can also be a lot of fun and present a challenge that can motivate the best and the brightest sport marketers.

Best Practice | **Adolph Coors Company Sports Sponsorship Criteria**

Here are Coors's criteria and rules for the Sports, CO-OP Events, Regional Events, and Special Marketing areas within the Field Marketing Department.

SPORTS

To qualify for sponsorship with Sports, subject sponsorship must meet the majority of the following guidelines:

1. Rank highly on the beer drinker index survey: participant, spectator, and viewer.

2. Score highly on the sports calculus: a calculation encompassing everything from size of audience to amount of product sold and retailer involvement opportunities.

3. Affect the bulk of the Coors marketing territory via on-site appearances.

4. Fulfill expectations or guarantee national media coverage.

5. Make sponsored individuals known and respected as "leaders" in their sport throughout the Coors market area, including media and spectators.

6. Create unique sponsored events that contain the possibility of Coors "ownership." They should be directed toward the target market and on the upswing in popularity, and they should provide the Coors distributors with an opportunity for tie-ins.

7. Lend the Sport to solid consumer promotion possibilities, especially outreach.

8. Lend the Sport to the process of continuity with meaningful reach, as well as optimal frequency.

9. Be controlled by a viable sanctioning body (e.g., NASCAR) that establishes or designates all events.

10. Ensure events of the sponsored party, known as venues, are competitive in nature.

CO-OP EVENTS (between Distributor and Brewery)

The following rules have been established by the CO-OP Administration to ensure uniform guidelines for all Coors distributors. These rules provide distributors and departments within the company a summary of the CO-OP Administration's operating latitude. Any questions not covered by these guidelines should be discussed with CO-OP Administration management.

1. Funding for programs must be shared on a 50 percent distributor/50 percent brewery basis.

2. Programs must have a minimum total cost of $1,000 to be considered for funding.

3. Programs must be in compliance with applicable laws and regulations.

4. Programs must conform to the company marketing plan, marketing strategy, and corporate image.

5. Programs must be submitted on the authorized CO-OP Event proposal form with enough information to allow for thorough analysis and evaluation.

6. Program proposals must be received by the area sales manager at least 30 days prior to the program start date, or 60 days if special graphics are required.

7. Proposals submitted after program completion may be declined.

8. Co-sponsorships with other beer companies are not allowed.

9. Use of Coors logo(s) for advertising, point-of-sale (P.O.S.), and merchandising items must be approved through the CO-OP Administration to qualify for funding.

10. Code 3 items associated with an event, such as special imprint streamers and banners, will be CO-OPed only after the distributor's Code 3 budget has been exhausted.

11. Funds should not be committed to programs that distributors would support in the absence of such funds. The intent of the CO-OP program is to encourage distributors' supplemental involvement to include, and go above and beyond, their local communities.

12. CO-OP Events will also participate in the following additional activities:
    a. Local trade shows
    b. Product/package introduction parties
    c. Free-standing hospitality at major sports events, excluding transportation, lodging, and tickets for retailers and beer. A minimum of 10,000 spectators at a sporting event—excluding fairs, festivals, show, etc.—are necessary to qualify.

13. The following will not be considered for CO-OP funding:
    a. Beer
    b. Direct mail
    c. Capital equipment
    d. Salaries, bonuses, and other benefits for Coors distributors' employees
    e. Sales incentive programs
    f. Dinners, banquets, and luncheons that are unrelated to an approved CO-OP event, including entertainment at those functions
    g. Gifts and donations, either money or goods
    h. Purchase of tickets by distributors for retailer use
    i. Transportation or lodging for retailers.

REGIONAL EVENTS: Fairs and Festivals

1. For the event to truly be a major regional event, it should draw a significant portion (i.e., 20%) of its attendance from outside the host distributor area.
2. Minimum attendance of 200,000 people (or 40,000 per day if it is less than a 5-day event).
3. Program cost to Coors of at least $10,000.
4. Distributor participation at a minimum of 30% and a maximum of 50% of the total cost.
5. Events must receive regional media coverage, specifically media coverage outside the event's metro area.
6. Beer sampling opportunities.
7. Priority states will receive preference, and the Sales and Brand will define priorities.
8. Non-sporting type events (e.g., fairs, festivals) will receive preference over sporting events (e.g., fights, runs).

REGIONAL EVENTS: Program Development

1. Regional: The program should affect a broad geographic area and population base.
2. Series: The program should execute multiple events in different locations to be conducted either simultaneously or over time.

3. Expandable: The program should be expandable and executable anywhere in the Coors market area.

4. High Participation: The program should be open to "mass participation" involving large participant and/or spectator numbers.

5. Have Continuity: The program should have potential for multiyear involvement and development by Coors.

6. Contract Executed: The program must be organized and executed by a bona fide professional promoter with whom Coors has a signed contract/sponsorship agreement.

7. Distributor Co-funded: The program must be at least 30% after the program's first year (T & D) of implementation.

SPECIAL MARKETING

Special Marketing will research, evaluate, and develop opportunities that match the young adult's lifestyle and brand objectives. The following profile of the young adult target applies to both Coors and Coors Light.

1. Demographic profile

Age: . . . . Primary target: LDA-24

Segments: . . . . Non-college, College

Sex: . . . . Primary target: Male
Secondary target: Female

Marital status: . . . . Single

Work status: . . . . (Ranked by priority)
Blue collar, white collar (gray collar)
Part-time, unemployed

Ethnic composition: . . . . . (ranked by opportunity) Anglo, Hispanic, Black

2. Demographic segmentation—college versus non-college: *

College	Non-college
LDA-26 (same mindset as LDA-24)	LDA-24 (25–29)
Male	Male (primary)
$8–12K year (blue collar influence)	$12–24K year
Single	Single
Anglo	Anglo
White/gray collar	Blue/gray collar

*It should be noted that Coors Brand planned to put emphasis on the non-college segment and Coors Light Brand planned to put emphasis on the college segment.

3. **Psychographic profile—descriptors characterize college versus non-college young adults**

College	Non-college
More likely to consume light beer	Followers
Direction oriented	Subject to heavy peer
More secure	Pressure
"Purpose in life"	"World owes me"
Party-women-music	Hedonistic
Somewhat serious minded (focused)	Anti-gay
"Live for today" (smaller degree)	Adventurous
Work hard, play hard	Smaller circle of friends
Self-centered	Macho
Health conscious	Not secure in self
Participant vs. spectator	Work ethic not important
Conservative (see limitations)	Cars important power symbols
Not moved by TV imagery	Fantasism/escapism
Not brand loyal	Look for acceptance
Peer pressure (jocks, Greeks, campus leaders)	"Live for today" ethic. Moved by TV imagery
Looking for uniqueness in life	Elusive
Takes safe choice	Party-women-music
Into high visibility items that identify self	Cynical

4. **Activities/recreation:**

College	Non-college
Intramural sports	Bar hopping
Parties	Hunting/fishing
Music (concerts, records, tapes)	Motorcycles/motor sports
Movies (high consumption)	Video games
Fraternities (B.M.O.C.)	Music (concerts financially restrictive)
Limited transportation	Movies
University sports (spectators)	TV-viewing at home
Entertainment within close locale	(MTV/rock videos)
Photography	Spectator sports (index higher)
Skiing	Y.M.C.A./recreation center oriented

Playing cards . . . . Local team participant
Swimming . . . . (e.g., golf, darts, softball,
bowling, basketball)

Tennis
Bowling
Weight lifting
Boating
Camping
Jogging
Racquetball

The following are examples of criteria that Coors uses to determine the relevance of a sales opportunity:

1. To what degree does the opportunity appeal to a young adult lifestyle (see previously listed profiles)?
2. How unique are the events?
3. Can the activities affect large groups of young adults on a major regional and/or national level?
4. Does the opportunity involve a 3-to-1 young adult ratio?
5. What entertainment activities, such as music and comedy, are available?
6. Is there an opportunity for brand dominance or ownership?
7. Are the programs cost effective and turnkey operative?
8. Are the activities fun and do they offer an escape from daily pressures?
9. Are the programs extensible through distributor efforts?
10. Are there cross-promotional opportunities available (if applicable)?
11. Do the events offer consistency and continuity within and between markets?
12. Is there an impact in a Coors marketing area where high concentrations of young adults reside?
13. Can the programs serve as vehicles for national and regional advertising and/or consumer promotion opportunities?

Sponsor Prospecting Worksheets

The worksheets guide the development of various sections of a sponsorship plan and cover potential prospects for sponsorship. Complete this worksheet as you would prepare a sponsorship plan.

Compile a list of all corporations that do business with you.

_____

_____

_____

_____

_____

_____

_____

Identify corporations through various information sources
(e.g., newspapers and journals) that may have an interest in
or connection to sport.

_____

_____

_____

_____

_____

_____

List specific candidates gathered from your Chamber of
Commerce search.

_____

_____

_____

_____

_____

_____

Report specific companies located from a review of the Yellow
Pages or from drive-by trips through the community.

_____

_____

_____

_____

_____

_____

Specify the most feasible point of contact for each potential sponsor that you have located.

_____

_____

_____

_____

_____

_____

3

Identifying Sponsor Needs

INTRODUCTION

As noted in Chapter 1, sponsorship in sport has been predicated on exchange theory with benefits accruing for sponsors and sport organizations alike. This chapter addresses the needs of the corporation. A quintessential need for any corporation is to differentiate itself from its competitors via a competitive advantage. A successful sport sponsorship may be an effective mechanism in creating and sustaining that advantage (Amis, Pant, & Slack, 1997).

SPONSOR RATIONALE

According to AT&T's vice president of advertising and communication, "It's no longer a world where company CEOs decide to sponsor their favorite sports at any cost. Sponsorships are business decisions that must go through the same profit and loss assessment as any other" (Graham, 1998, p. 34). This point was further reinforced by Michael Payne, former IOC marketing director, who said that "corporation bosses are increasingly having to justify their marketing investments to their shareholders and can no longer just say being associated with the Olympics is good for a company—they will have to prove it with hard facts" ("Keeping the Olympics' Ideal," 1997, p. 32). One of the best clarifications of what sponsors are looking for in their relationships with sport organizations was forwarded by Donna Lopiano (cited in Reynolds, 1998, p. 30): "Sponsorships have to measure up on a performance basis in their ability to match the right demographic and psychographic targets, reach the appropriate decision makers and ultimately help move product or services" In the end, sponsorship consultant Kim Skildum-Reid (2008a, p. 8) best summarized the point by saying, "It's time to get over yourself! Sponsors don't want to align with you, they want to align with their target market. So stop making the proposal about your need, your profile, and your general fabulosity," she wrote in her blog. "Start by talking about how you are a conduit for that sponsor to really connect with—not just get in front of—the target market."

CORPORATE CRITERIA FOR SPONSOR EVALUATION

According to Ukman (2004a, p. vii), "Talk to any four sponsors of any property and you will find that, while they are sponsoring the same property, each is using sponsorship to accomplish different objectives." For example, banks may be interested in new customer acquisition and business-to-business (B2B) relationships, while automotive sponsors may be looking to showcase new models and drive floor traffic. The criteria used by sponsors in their evaluation of proposals have been discussed extensively in the literature. Many corporations have developed definitive criteria, while others are more subjective.

Perhaps the most comprehensive study of corporate criteria was Irwin, Assimakopoulos, and Sutton's (1994) initial foray into sponsorship research, which produced a useful model for corporations to evaluate sponsorship proposals. Their model presented an array of factors for comparison (p. 59):

Budget considerations	Event management
Affordability	Event profile
Tax benefits	Organizing committee
Position/Image	Media guarantees
Product-sport image fit	Legal status
Product utility fit	Governing body status
Image-target fit	Marketing agency profile
Targeting of market	Integrated communications
Extended media coverage	Extended audience
Immediate audience	Public relations/publicity
Competition consideration	Sales promotions
Competition's interest	Personal selling
Ambush market avoidance	Strategies
Level of involvement	Type of sponsorship
Title sponsor	Established
Major sponsor	New
Cosponsor	Team
In-kind sponsor	League/Championship
Exclusivity	Event
Long-term involvement	Facility
Once-off	

Further research was conducted to test the validity of their model. They found that the factors that were rated as most important fit between sport image and product/service image, target market fit, demographic profile of the extended audience, demographic fit of the immediate audience, and opportunities for signage (Irwin, Assimakopoulos, & Sutton, 1994). Additional research by Thwaites and Aguilar-Manjarrez (1997) found that community involvement and enhancement of the company image were highly rated, as well. Their study also found that corporate hospitality and building trade relations were considered to be important factors for companies seeking sport sponsorships. In addition, a considerable amount of research has shown that market-driven objectives, such as increased market share, new client acquisition, new product awareness, and on-site sales have been cited as critical factors (Copeland, Frisby, & McCarville, 1996;

Irwin & Sutton, 1994; Kuzma, Shanklin, & McCally, 1993). Stotlar's (1999) research and Seaver's (2004) study of 50 leading U.S. sport sponsors revealed that sales and market-specific objectives were considered the most critical components in a sponsorship partnership. Corporate executives rated three items above all other factors: the ability to create new customers, increase sales quantifiably, and tie-in to the current marketing strategy. Ukman (2008) identified the top five sponsorship objectives as follows: increase brand loyalty, increase awareness, change/reinforce image, and drive retail sales. Obviously, there is considerable agreement across the industry. Several industry-based examples are illustrated below.

Reebok/adidas sponsorship executives expect certain sponsorship elements in event sponsorships, including on-site and local retailer sales activities, product expos and new product sampling, promotions of their national account representatives, sponsored athlete clinics and autograph sessions, scheduled press receptions, course signage and banners, national network coverage, and hospitality/VIP accommodations. Volvo, a long-time sport sponsor, forwarded additional thoughts regarding its sponsorship decisions. Through its ups and downs with tennis, Volvo's position was that a company should make large investments to achieve more brand name exposure while at the same time requiring relatively less work. The Volvo philosophy also indicated that a long-term commitment for three to five years was more beneficial.

One of the basic criteria involved in matching sport organizations with sponsors is to establish a demographic fit between the sport organization's participant/audience base and the target market of the sponsor. For instance, the out-board engine manufacturer Evinrude sponsors several fishing tournaments. The VP of sales and marketing said, "We are able to have a presence in front of enthusiastic anglers nearly year-round, and anglers are one of our most important markets" ("Evinrude Renews," 2004). It's all about connecting with their target audience.

Economic factors are also a key element in a sponsor-event match. Investment firm Charles Schwab and Co. signed on to sponsor the Professional Golfers' Association of America (PGA) Tour as title sponsor of the Charles Schwab Cup. Not only can Schwab entertain high-income clients through its hospitality program, but they also provide investment-related services to PGA players and staff. The match seems better than if they were to sponsor action sports where fans and participants typically have less discretionary funds to invest. Companies sponsoring action sports are often looking to capture the elusive young consumer in order to influence lifelong brand loyalty. Age represents one of the demographic variables in which sponsors may be interested, but gender may surface as another critical factor. While some corporations focus on a predominately male demographic, "companies are waking up to the power of marketing to women" (www.pgatour.com). Selecting the right fit with the sponsor on this variable is equally important.

When addressing demographics, the sport marketer should be sure to elaborate on how a sponsor can benefit from targeting a particular group. For example, convincing a sponsor that the demographic composition of an event is a good match with the corporation's target market is only the first step. The sport marketer, for instance, can make their database available for the sponsor's use in direct marketing. The National Athletic Trainers Association allows sponsors to access its 20,000 bi-monthly emails, noting, "If sponsors want to get a message out, we want them to use every communications piece we have available" ("Five Key Factors," 2004, p. 3). Similarly, Dick's Sporting Goods secured sponsorship with Little League Baseball in 2008 to capture expenditures on sporting goods from this lucrative demographic, which allowed sponsoring corporations to mail advertising messages directly to 3 million Little League players. For a full presentation of their sponsors, check out www.littleleague.org/learn/partnerships/sponsors.htm.

There has, however, been an outcry that these actions result in an overcommercialization of youth sport. In an effort to reduce such protests, the American Youth Soccer Organization performs direct mailing for sponsors so they can screen any potentially offensive material. Although access to a sport organization's database can make a proposal more enticing, it may be more ethical to limit sponsors' use of mailing lists to include only consenting adult constituents (opt-ins). Remember, their personal information belongs to them, not to you.

Understanding and affecting consumer psychographics—the attitudes, beliefs and feelings of consumers—is also important to companies engaged in sponsorship. In this light, the U.S. Army was very active in a variety of racing programs sponsoring vehicles in both the National Hot Rod Association (NHRA) and NASCAR. The psychographic profile of those fans, and the ability to set up displays with Hummers, tanks and a climbing wall, enhanced their ability to attract new recruits. However, under pressure from Congress, none of the armed forces continued their motorsports sponsorships in 2013 (Long, 2012).

Loyalty patterns are also extremely important to sponsors: Data have indicated that about 73% of NASCAR fans choose the products of their sport's sponsors over others. Data show that NASCAR fans were three times more likely to purchase a sponsor's product over a similar product from a nonsponsor ("Race Fans," 2012). Pitts (Pitts & Stotlar, 2013) also found high consumer loyalty in her study of Gay Games sponsors, determining that 68% of participants recognized sponsors and that 74% of attendees intended to purchase from sponsors. The gay and lesbian market represents a $743 billion market (SDGLN Staff, 2010).

As one author noted, "It is theoretically possible to put up the money to sponsor an event, hang a big billboard at the event, and have that be the end of it. But any organization that looked on sponsorship in this limited fashion would be foolish indeed" (Hagstrom, 1998, p. 51). Skildum-Reid (2012) noted that sponsorship partnerships are less about signage and more about returning value to the sponsors while enhancing the overall game experience. She also said (Skildum-Reid (2008b, p. 7), "I'm not saying that you need to ditch all of your signage, just stop talking about it. The more effort you put into how-big-is-my-logo and where-is-my–banner, the less you will focus on the truly strategic aspects of sponsorship." Thus, sponsors can profit from an array of benefits attainable through sport sponsorship. To complement the research findings in this area, additional cases are presented that highlight corporate objectives in commonly cited categories; specifically, they are *awareness, image, sales, hospitality,* and *employee motivation.*

Awareness Objectives

Understanding sponsor rationale regarding awareness has a lot to do with television. The question arises: What do the 20 official sponsors and suppliers of the World Cup hope to get from their involvement? Not just exposure to 2.5 million ticket holders. They're after a piece of the 36 billion cumulative television audience. Similarly, PGA Tour events are after the "Tiger Factor," where, even after his scandal, television ratings and shares increase on average 21%, or about 2 million viewers, if Tiger Woods is in the tournament and contending for the title.

An important aspect of sport sponsorship that cannot be overlooked for the coming decade is the aspect of globalization. In a world economy, companies may find it difficult to communicate to consumers in Zimbabwe or China, but a sport sponsorship can help cut through some of the existing barriers. For example, UPS, a worldwide sponsor of the 2008 and 2012 Olympic Games, viewed Olympic sponsorship as an opportunity to deepen international business contacts and hoped to reap benefits from these contacts in future business dealings. Many corporations are also capitalizing on the international success of sports like the NBA, where not only do U.S. players now have high levels of global recognition, but the increasing percentage of international players in the NBA make their endorsements increasingly valuable. UPS extended its sponsorship activities for Beijing by also contracting with the Chinese Basketball Association to capitalize on the popularity of players like Yao Ming and Yi Jianlian. Another interesting sponsorship with global implications came when language tutorial company Rosetta Stone hired Olympic gold medalist Michael Phelps as a spokesperson while he learned Chinese for the 2008 Games (Mickle, 2008a).

The awareness objective can still be effective even if relatively few consumers know anything about the sponsor's product or company; however, it has been shown to do little for a company like Coca-Cola. John Cordova (1996), senior business manager for Coca-Cola, referred to event signage as "wallpaper." In the 1980s, Coke's advertising motto was "If it stands still, paint it red, if it moves, sponsor it." This be-everywhere strategy has been replaced by *consumer activation*. In addition, its internal research showed that stadium signage did not drive product sales. Coke found that there was not enough profit from in-stadium product sales to justify large sponsorship expenditures. Furthermore, even pouring rights in the stadium were of marginal value; Coke found that the ridiculously high prices charged by some sport concessionaires were being blamed on Coke (Cordova, 1996). A similar note was sounded by Miller Brewing Company's director of sport marketing when he said, "The strategy is much more than how much signage we get. Visibility is not the key for us. Everyone knows who Miller is, but we need inventory that makes the brand come alive" (Lauletta, 2003, p. 8).

Additional support concerning the tenuous value of awareness came from Former Nike Marketing Vice President Steve Miller when he indicated that Nike did not factor exposure of its logo into sponsorship valuation. He believed that if people didn't recognize a Swoosh, the famous Nike logo, before the sponsorship, they never would. With college sponsorships, Nike has been more interested in how much product the partnership could sell at retail. This was the underpinning of Nike's 20+ year relationship (replaced by adidas in 2008) with the University of Michigan, one of the top selling licensed collegiate brands in the last decade . Nike secured sponsorship of sport programs at the United States Air Force Academy (USAFA), but not only for the television exposure garnered through the Air Force football team's televised games and Bowl appearances. They were actually more attracted to the $5 million a year in merchandise sales through the USAFA visitor's center, 33% of which was based off of Nike product. Sport marketing executives Amshay and Brian (1998) summarized the issue, stating, "Exposure has value, but it is hugely overrated" (p. 23).

Image Objectives

A company's image is the sum of beliefs, ideas, and impressions held by consumers about the company and its products (Ries & Trout, 1986). Given this, research has shown that sport sponsorship can help shape an otherwise obscure corporate image, but it can do little to change one. Skildum-Reid (2008a, p. 5) says that "properties cannot give a sponsor an image that they don't authentically have. They can only support, extend, or underpin an existing attribute." This was exemplified when Kmart Corporation sponsored various PGA golf events in an attempt to elevate its image by tying it to an upscale event. The strategy was not, however, very successful. "Hugo Boss has been an International Sponsor of Davis Cup since 1987, providing clothing to teams, VIPs, officials, event staff, and ball kids," ("Hugo Boss," 2007, para. 1) and according to Hugo Boss's director of communications, "tennis perfectly conveys the qualities of elegance, success and cosmopolitanism embodied by Hugo Boss" (para. 1).

This component can be observed in a variety of settings. Rolex does not sponsor rodeo events and Wrangler Jeans does not sponsor yachting. McDonald's research (1998) supported the benefits of matching the image of the sport with the image of the corporation. His research confirmed that a sponsorship was more effective if there was a high level of congruence between the image of the sport and that of the company. He evaluated the concepts of perceptual fit around the terms *sophisticated*, *rugged*, *exciting*, and *wholesome*. His research concluded that the creation of a good perceptual fit between the sport event and the sponsoring company could contribute to brand equity for the sponsor (McDonald, 1998).

An excellent overview of the sponsorship of the New Zealand Rugby Union's All Blacks by adidas is provided by Motion, Leitch, and Brodie (2003; see additional readings). Following McDonald's observation (above), the key attributes of the All Blacks were determined to be *power, masculinity, commitment, teamwork, New Zealand, tradition*, and *inspirational* (Motion et al., 2003, p. 1087). "When adidas evaluates a potential partner they look for two or three matching brand values present in their make-up or in the style in which they take part in sport. The values of 'tradition' and 'New Zealand' were matched to the adidas value of 'authentic'" (Motion et al., 2003, p. 1087). The authors summarized that "adidas and the All Blacks brand values were compatible and connected at a fundamental level" (Motion et al., 2003, p. 1090).

Sales Objectives

Sales objectives include such factors as increasing the sales levels of certain brands and getting people to sample a product. In most of the recent research on corporate criteria, the sales factor ranks near the top of the list in important considerations for corporations looking to engage in sport sponsorship (Stotlar, 1999). Steve Saunders (1996), former marketing vice president at Coors, said that the bottom line for a Coors sport sponsorship is always, "Does it sell beer?" To illustrate the point, consider the case of Coors's association with the Colorado Rockies baseball team. At Coors Field, Coors has a microbrewery from which it bottles and sells specialty beer in the stadium and the general market. It also sells a significant volume of beer during the 81 home games and other events at Coors Field. Within the same industry, former Anheuser-Busch VP for Sport Marketing Tony Ponturo (2002) said, "It's not our goal to be a sponsor, our goal is to sell our product."

In assessing the value of Coors involvement, Saunders (1996) added that the days of "playing calculus" are over. His reference to calculus explained how, in previous years, Coors has utilized a formula to calculate a summative value of X dollars for a stadium sign, X dollars for pouring rights, X dollars per impression (i.e., $.05 per spectator), and X dollars for title to the event. In Saunders's view, corporate valuation will be based on the ability of an event to sell beer on site, to increase market share, and to provide direct product profits through Coors distributors.

For many companies engaged in retail sales, floor traffic equates to increased sales. Therefore, in a very successful arrangement with Wendy's restaurants, the United States Association for Blind Athletes (USABA) created the SportMates program. Through this sponsorship, Wendy's would make a donation to the USABA for each designated combo meal sold. This promotion resulted in a one-month sales increase of 34.5% for Colorado Wendy's outlets and enabled Wendy's to raise $25,000 for the USABA. In another case, Mercedes-Benz sponsored one of the top professional tennis tours (ATP) for 12 years ending in 2008, yet as a result, Mercedes was able to sell over 150 cars to tournament players. They also offered promotions in tournament host cities that created significant floor traffic and test drives. A combination of the two proved to be a very successful strategy for Mercedes.

Adidas signed up with the Royal and Ancient golf course in St. Andrews Scotland as its official supplier. Not only does adidas outfit all of the staff during its tournaments, but it also has exclusive sales of apparel from the pro shop. Although the numbers are not available, it can be assumed that a large portion of visitors to the birthplace of golf would take home a golf shirt as a souvenir. Similarly, sportswear company Champion, owned by Hanes brands, signed up for title sponsorship of the ESPN Wide World of Sports stadium, part of the Disney World complex, to promote Disney. But they also saw an opportunity for exclusive sales rights to clothing sold at the venue as well as all Disney parks and resorts.

Product sampling has also been an effective sponsorship tool by assisting sponsors in attracting potential consumers. U.S. Swimming and Johnson & Johnson's Sundown

Sunscreen products implemented one such example: their sponsorship agreement provided that Johnson & Johnson send sample packets of sunscreen to over 2000 local swim clubs for distribution at area swim meets. This met one of the primary objectives of the company—to get the product into the hands of the most likely customers; and who better than young swimmers and their families?

Product sampling continually generates a great deal of interest in the product, and sales can be tracked to indicate an overall effect on sales. It also has been shown to be effective in developing consumer loyalty and providing the company with reliable feedback on products with minimal costs.

Service companies can also generate sales through sport sponsorship. Here, sponsorship strategies focus not only on effective sales, but also on customer acquisition objectives as primary criteria. In addition, another sport executive also commented that the "focus should not be strictly on exposure, but [be] more sales driven" (Seaver, 1996, p. 33). According to a recent industry survey, a sponsor was quoted as saying, "It's real simple. Ultimately, what we have to do is to sell product. A banner ad does not cut it. We need to know that our involvement sold something" (Seaver, 2004, p. 17). One director of sponsorships said, "We are no longer satisfied with enhanced image; give us opportunities for on-site sales . . . dealer tie-ins and we'll listen" (Seaver, 1996, p. 34).

Thus, the relationship between sport organizers and sponsors has evolved to accentuate *return on investment* (ROI). As a worldwide sponsor of the Olympic Games, General Electric was able to use its business associations with the 2008 Beijing Olympic Games to secure $153 million in construction and infrastructure projects in its first two years of the sponsorship. Irwin and Sutton's research (1994) on corporate criteria found that market-driven objectives, such as increasing sales and market share, were highly rated criteria in sponsorship selection. Calculated value assessment replaced other factors as the primary strategy employed by both event owners and sponsors during the 1990s and is a mainstay of the sponsorship industry.

In support of this transition, the top ranked criterion in Seaver's (2004) industry survey was "a program with the ability to drive quantifiable sales into area retailers"—76% of participants ranked it as extremely important and 20% cited it as important. Xerox personified this concept in its Olympic sponsorship campaigns by carefully tracking sales records, which revealed 35,000 leads and the sale of more than 6,000 copiers directly attributable to its Olympic strategy and marketing initiatives (Stotlar, 1997).

Reebok/adidas has also emphasized the sales aspect when it evaluates road-race sponsorships. They have prioritized events in which they can sell product at the race site or, alternatively, involve local Reebok retailers. In another example, the CEO of Ranger fishing boats, sponsor of several bass fishing tournaments (FLW Tour, www.flwoutdoors.com/sponsors.cfm), said sponsorship is not about delivering a million impressions but about getting the message to someone who is going to buy a $20,000 boat in the next 12 months. The clear message is that helping a sponsor move product can develop deeper revenue. Coca-Cola's Cordova said, "Bring me a promotion that will put a Coke in the hands of a 12 year old and we can work a deal" (Cordova, 1996).

Hospitality Objectives

Sponsors need places and events to use for entertaining potential clients and enhancing business-to-business relationships (B2B). Sporting events have, for many years, provided great opportunities for this activity. NASCAR has been one of the more successful sports in leveraging its popularity through hospitality activities. First, all of the racetracks offer corporate suites in conjunction with sponsorship packages. At Darlington International Raceway, the suites have been priced at $200,000 and have attracted companies like Interstate Batteries, Pepsi, and DuPont. DuPont, which sponsors Jeff Gordon's Hendrick Motorsports racecar, typically entertains up to 2,000 clients, employees, and associates at a single event, taking them on tours of the pits, providing them a fabulous meal, and letting them visit with Jeff Gordon prior to moving up to their suite to watch the race. At the Colonial golf tournament, sponsor Crown Plaza brought in 1,000 of its top clients to its skybox and invited 40 VIPs, so-called high-value clients, to extend their stay and play the course the day after the tournament. Similar tactics were in place at the America's Cup sailing races where some sponsors hired yachts to cruise the racecourse while conducting hospitality events. Hospitality does not come cheap, however. At the 2012 U.S. Open in golf at the Olympic Club, a tent in the sponsor village started at $235,000 for 50 guests and went to $750,000 for a more sophisticated clubhouse location. Similarly, hospitality prices at the Masters ran about $6,000 per person. These prices only include the space to entertain and typically do not provide food or beverage services (Smith, 2012).

Hospitality is often referred to as B2B marketing. This is where businesses can develop relationships with their best customers. It's about influence and what the industry refers to as creating a *network* position. FedEx uses its relationship with the NFL to provide hospitality events in stadiums on nongame days. These events provide controlled sales environments that capitalize on the draw of the team. They also give FedEx an experience that the typical fan cannot buy—NFL Open Houses at stadiums on nongame days, where "hundreds of FedEx's best customers are invited to go onto the field, into the locker rooms, hear about FedEx service and meet a running back or quarterback" (Odell, 2012, "You Can't Own Everything" section, para. 4). In 2012 the Dallas Cowboys began packaging unique experiences with their sponsorships. Included were things like a seat in the "war room" during draft day, shadowing a reporter on the sidelines, and even a tryout slot with the Dallas Cowboy Cheerleaders (Kaplan, 2012).

UPS, working with IMG College, utilizes its sponsorship with 62 colleges and universities to highlight its services. At least for one game per season, a local UPS driver is selected to deliver the game ball and the driver's family is treated to VIP treatment and tickets at the game (Spanberg, 2012b).

Employee Morale Objectives

One established method of increasing employee morale is to involve famous athletes in corporate affairs. Olympic swimmer Michael Phelps was one of Visa's sponsored athletes for 2008 and 2012. They used Phelps in a variety of ads and promotions during the interval between Games. Visa has also successfully used its Olympic sponsorship to build team spirit within the corporation. One of its techniques was to make Olympic logo golf shirts available to all employees. During the lead up to the Games, they had to reorder shirts five different times because of the high demand ("Olympic Games Media Kit," n.d.).

Discover Financial Services also uses its sport sponsorship for employee morale. As a sponsor of the NHL, Discover was able to bring the Stanley Cup won by the Chicago Blackhawks in 2012 for a display at its corporate offices in Chicago. Over 1,000 employees came to see and pose with the Cup (Spanberg, 2012b).

Other Sponsor Objectives

Additional criteria upon which companies make sponsorship decisions include other current sponsors and mix of products, corporate relations with other sponsors; cooperation from the host facility for signage, access, and placement; and the potential for VIP contacts. An outline of the sponsorship needs examined by Anheuser-Busch is presented in Figure 3.1.

Season Tickets
  a. Complimentary
  b. Discount
  c. Full purchase availability

Reserved Seat Tickets
  a. Complimentary
  b. Discount
  c. Full purchase availability

General Admission Tickets
  a. Complimentary
  b. Discount
  c. Full-purchase availability
  d. Blocks for charity use
  e. Scoreboard mention
  f. Invitations

Special Stadium Nights
  a. Free tickets
  b. Special meeting room
  c. Souvenirs/programs
  d. First-ball ceremony

Use of On-Air Talent
  a. Lead-ins
  b. Drop-in
  c. Live announcer
  d. Special promo spots
  e. No charge
  f. Charge (amount)
  g. Re-use off station
       On-camera
       Off-camera

Yearbook/Press Guide/Program/Scorecard Ads
  a. Complimentary
  b. Discount purchase
  c. Full purchase
  d. Number of complimentary copies

Arena Signage
  a. Availability
  b. Number
  c. Complimentary
  d. Charge (amount)

Special Items
  a. Use of VIP rooms
  b. Use of luxury box
  c. League/press passes
  d. Parking passes
  e. Ticket purchase option
  f. Use of highlight film
  g. Use of product music
  h. Merchandising
  i. Sampling opportunity

Scoreboard/Public Address Exposure in Stadium
  a. Copy only
  b. Copy and art
  c. Number of times per game
  d. Complimentary
  e. Discount purchase

Participation in Events
  a. Pre-game
  b. Half time
  c. On-field or on-floor
  d. Presentations

Figure 3.1. Anheuser-Busch Sports Sponsorship Evaluation

The number of events and their geographic representation are also key elements in sponsor decisions. The International Events Group has clarified the difference between national and regional events. Ukman (2004b) indicated that to be considered a *national* event, the sponsorship impact would need to affect 15 major markets. Otherwise, it should be classified as a regional event. Major companies that have national or international distribution channels are always interested in wholesaler tie-ins. This typically relates to the ability of a local distributor to have special promotions, on-site displays, and possibly cooperative advertising. Some corporations are also drawn to sport sponsorship by the potential for merchandising. Miller Brewing Company sells facsimile jackets and T-shirts to supplement their NASCAR racing program. Miller not only realizes substantial profits from the products themselves, but increases its visibility and extends its influence into the local community for periods far in excess of the race day (store.nascar.com).

Activation

The power of relevant activation cannot be overlooked. Sponsors need to communicate with each of the audiences in meaningful ways. Simply throwing up a sign and putting the sponsor's logo in the game program won't work. Coca-Cola uses its sponsorship of the Olympic Games to extend its reach into the community by also sponsoring the Olympic Torch Relay. Coca-Cola is more involved in communities by selecting local Coke bottlers to participate in nominating Olympic torch runners. In 2008, the first time the torch traveled internationally, Coke activated its sponsorship across China, Africa, and throughout the international route of the torch. Although the Torch Relay met with some international protest, based on China's stance on Tibetan independence, the local activation efforts were a success.

Coke used another activation strategy when it took over sponsorship of the NHRA with its PowerAde brand; as title sponsor, Coke wanted to connect with racing fans. It launched a special flavor of its sport drink called "NHRA PowerAde" after field testing and online research with NHRA fans.

In another Olympic-related sponsorship, Visa was able to activate its card usage through member banks by offering sweepstakes for trips to the Games. At one bank sweepstakes, every transaction with a Visa card qualified as an entry into the drawing, and as a result, bank revenues increased 300% over a control group during the 60-day promotion ("Staying Ahead of the Games," 2004). At Turner Field in Atlanta, sponsorship with the area Lexus dealers provided reserved parking for Lexus owners. BMW also activated its sponsorship with American Ski Corporation, owner of seven ski resorts, by supplying hotel guests with the courtesy of BMW sport utility vehicles—the program generated 15,000 test drives. At the higher levels, BMW invited 150 of its best customers for expense-paid ski vacations. In New Zealand, cereal maker Weet-Bix sponsored a face-recognition website where kids could go online and match a player on the All Blacks rugby team to their own faces (Skildum-Reid, 2008c). It was tremendously successful. These types of activation strategies bring the customer directly in touch with the benefits of sponsorship.

Industry data have shown that a lot of sponsors are not spending enough money on activation. Performance Research (2004) found that 70% of sponsors are spending less than the suggested $3-to-$1 on activation. The industry average was only $1.75 for each dollar spent. Former MasterCard Vice President of Global Sponsorships and Event Marketing Bob Cramer commented, "We are talking about activation with more and more of our partners. We are looking at activation like inventory, and properties need to do the same. It is a hard pill for properties to swallow because it is not so much about what they can do for us at the event but in the marketplace" (Migala, 2004, p. 2). The sponsorship director for Janus commented about sponsoring the New York City Triathlon: "Half of the properties we work with expect us to create our own programs, pay for them, and implement them completely on our own. They want us to pay a sponsorship fee and they leave all of the activation up to the sponsor. In concept that might work, but in reality it usually doesn't. We have to do things in tandem to make sure things work smoothly" ("Sponsors Identify," 2008, p. 1). Another example of corporate integration on sponsorship activities can be seen with the FedEx example in the Best Practice section of this chapter.

Another emerging activation follows the marketing trend of *experience marketing*. Though sponsorship corporations are looking for ways to relate to their products and enhance their experience with the event, sponsors will look for an individual, event, club, or organization in the sports arena that carries a sufficiently high level of emotional involvement with their target audience. Furthermore, "sponsorship must motivate consumers to interact with the sponsor's product—whether that's touching it, using it, speaking to a specialist about it, etc.—and have them walk away with more knowledge about it" ("Product Integration," 2004, p. 3).

U.S. Open tennis sponsor American Express implemented an excellent activation through experience marketing campaign in 2012. Not only had American Express secured individual sponsorship agreements with world-number 1 Victoria Azarenka and rising star Carolina Wozniacki, but as a tournament sponsor, they had a 20,000 square-foot exhibition center. That facility hosted American Express's Fan Experience where kids could play tennis games on a Wii and XBox Kinect and others could hit balls on an indoor practice court. Adults could even have their swing analyzed through computer software. Because of seriously inclement weather, the indoor center became a very popular attraction. Further activation was seen as AmEx partnered with apparel sponsor Ralph Lauren so that if an attendee spent $150 on RL apparel using their AmEx card, they would get a $50 gift card (Wall-Doe, 2012).

These experiences will, in turn, increase consumer purchase intentions and generate positive brand associations. While including these elements creates added benefits, the situation should not be left to chance. The extent and level of integration should be formalized in the contract and should note the specific activities that will ensure success.

An excellent example of integration occurred in Sprint's sponsorship of NASCAR. Sprint created FanScan In-Car Audio, a wireless service that connects fans with the live communications between drivers and pits during the race. "Sprint's affiliation with NASCAR is based entirely on how we can leverage our core competencies in wireless communication to enhance the fan experience" (www .nascar.com/news/121126/champions-week-schedule/index .html, p. 6).

Anheuser-Busch is testing a new activation at several NFL stadiums. Because A-B has an association with 28 NFL teams, it has a wide base of support. The program uses downloadable apps to allow spectators to access team content (stats, proprietary videos, team photos, virtual

> In the end, the goal of activation is to increase the fan's affinity toward and "stickiness" with the sponsor's brand. This means affecting the consumer's perception and behavior toward the brand.

stadium tours, etc.). However, to activate the app, fans must scan a Bud Light image from stadium signage or other collateral material. This is clearly a new form of activation that merits consideration as fans move to second-screen technology (Lefton, 2012b).

Cross-Promotion

Cross-promotion, the ability of sponsors to work cooperatively in a sponsorship, has been noted to be "among the most powerful and popular activation methods as they can grant marketers access to new distribution channels and spread out promotional costs across multiple partners" ("Five Key Factors," 2004, p. 3). For example, NASCAR put together a B2B council to help sponsors work together more closely, and to cooperate on a variety of hospitality and activation strategies. Another successful cross-promotion strategy was created by the NHL Florida Panthers. They developed a partner-only website where its business partners could network and work on promotions among themselves, increasing the value of the involvement with the team (Talalay, 2008).

In the sport of fishing, sponsors of a series of fishing tournaments banded together to package their products for participants and spectators that included Evinrude outboard motors, Ranger fishing boats, and EverStart Marine Batteries in the "Ultimate Fishing Package" ("Evinrude Renews," 2004). In another cross-promotion, Olympic partner Coca-Cola persuaded one of the athletes it sponsors, Olympic wrestler Shane Hamman, to spend a day at fellow sponsor 24 Hour Fitness working out with a lucky employee and gym member who won an in-store contest. As part of the contest, 24 Hour Fitness, in turn, promoted Coca-Cola's PowerAde line of sports drinks.

Sponsors are also motivated by the type and amount of press coverage, both print and electronic, that they receive as a result of the sponsorship. Sport organizations can utilize data collected from previous events, or from similar events if a new event is proposed, to convince sponsors there is a sufficient media value returned through the sponsorship program. The data could include Facebook likes, Twitter followers, column inches that appeared in the newspaper, and airtime of news or special reports related to the event on the Web, television, and radio.

The timing of an event can also play an important role in sport sponsorship. Companies continually introduce new products and services to the market. A growing number of cruise lines are using sport sponsorship to promote new cruise activities, like climbing walls and adventure side-trips. Airlines are adding new cities to their routes, and tying an event into a new destination can prove to be advantageous for the airline.

In addition, seasonal timing should be examined. Automobile dealers typically introduce the new model year in the fall, which coincides with football season and could create a great opportunity for new products to be displayed at games. In another example, computer game maker EA Sports has sponsored the Maui Invitational basketball tournament. This tournament has featured the nation's top collegiate teams and falls at the beginning of the holiday shopping season in late November. Circumstances like these create enormous opportunities for sport marketers as new companies look for effective strategies to promote their new identity.

Details surrounding an event's organizing committee are also important to potential sponsors. The event organizers should be well prepared and financially stable, with a proven record of organizing other activities. Sponsors are always going to be cautious about lending their name and corporate identity to another entity; therefore, attention to stability and professionalism is imperative.

Sponsors are also wary of the multitude of risks that may be associated with an event. The potential for a public relations disaster should be tolerable. There are always risks, some dealing with the weather (like the 2012 ING New York City Marathon cancelled by Hurricane Sandy), but the organizers should be willing to point out potential risks to the sponsor. One specific example illustrates this point. When Dodge trucks became involved in the sponsorship of the Iditarod, a major dog sled race, they were unaware that the public relations generated from animal rights activists could produce a substantial amount of negative press coverage and controversy. Similar risks can be found with rodeo events. As a preemptive maneuver to offset such a controversy, the Professional Rodeo Cowboys Association published a brochure on the protections and humane treatment of animals that sponsors can use to explain the activities and defend its events.

Sometimes even the type of sponsorship can cause controversy. In 2004, the Daytona Cubs, a Triple A baseball team, conducted a funeral giveaway to the best essay on a fan's ideal funeral. The program was sponsored by a local funeral home but caused many in the community to be upset over what they considered to be the trivialization of death ("Baseball's Cubs Run Free Funeral Promotion," 2004).

Cause-Related Sponsorship

One of the most significant trends in sport marketing is to affiliate a sport sponsorship with a popular cause. Muellner (1998) noted, "Without a doubt, there are a lot more companies trying to market with cause-related endeavors" (p. 8). The rationale for involvement in cause-related marketing is clear when a more detailed look at consumer response is considered. Irwin, Lackowitz, Cornwell, and Clark (2003, p. 138) noted that "it is critical that the CRM [cause-related marketing] tie-in be viewed as valuable and genuine to the consumer. They noted that 83% of consumers developed a more positive impression of companies engaged in CRM." Several examples of this practice can be detected throughout the sport industry (also refer to Chapter 1).

Started in 1996, an event was developed to honor the late college basketball coach Jim Valvano and raise money for cancer research. The college basketball tournament entitled "Coaches vs. Cancer" raises over $1,000,000 each year. Another example is the

Terry Fox Run to raise funds to fight cancer, which began in 1995. This event has been held in more than 50 countries and has been one of the most ambitious international cause-related sporting events. Furthermore, The Susan G. Komen Race for the Cure represents another very popular running event held annually in numerous communities across the U.S. to raise money for breast cancer research. Race for the Cure raises over $80 million annually, the majority of which stays in the host communities.

October has been recognized as Cancer Awareness Month and the NFL players and officials continually show support. Their support is most visible through the pink accessories worn during the games. The NBA also has its ties to charity with the "NBA Cares" program. NBA Cares is the league's global community outreach initiative that addresses important social issues such as education, youth and family development, and health and wellness. The NBA and its teams support a range of programs, partners, and initiatives that strive to positively impact children and families worldwide. In the aftermath of Hurricane Sandy in New York, NBA Cares organized a food and clothing campaign for the victims.

"Studies support the notion that consumers feel better about a brand they believe is contributing to society" (Muellner, 1998, p. 8). An IEG sponsorship report (Ukman, 2004c) indicated that "nearly half of Americans are engaged in some form of consumer activation," causing buying decisions to rest on the social actions of the companies from which they purchase products (p. 2). Furthermore, "the more affluent the consumer, as well as the more highly-educated, the more they participated in consumer activism" (p. 2). Their research also showed that 78% of consumers would buy from a sponsoring company that was associated with a worthy cause about which they cared. In addition, 66% reported they would switch brands, 62% would switch retailers, and 54% said they would pay more (5–10%) for items offered by a company that was involved with an important cause (Ukman, 1997a, p. 2). Consumers were equally perturbed at companies that lacked a viable philanthropy program. More than 50% of consumers had actually boycotted products from companies that were not active in social programs. Despite all of the success, some degree of caution must be exercised in cause-related marketing campaigns. One marketing executive noted, "If something is done purely for publicity, people see through it—it has to come from a motivation to work for the betterment of the community" (Muellner, 1998, p. 8).

GRASSROOTS (COMMUNITY-BASED) SPONSORSHIP

Grassroots sponsorship brings marketing to a local community or region as opposed to a national scope. Pepsi modified its strategy for multicultural sport marketing in 2004 by opting to spread its dollars across a greater number of small events with focused ethnic profiles ("Pepsi Wants," 2004). Previous research has shown that several factors evident in national sponsorship selection were the same as those for sponsoring grassroots sport; most notably, increasing corporate exposure and consumer awareness were present in both national and local sponsorship. Another advantage of grassroots sport sponsorship includes increased availability for product sampling and prototype testing as additional ways to reach consumers. Greenwald and Fernandez-Balboa (1998) noted that, in grassroots sport sponsorship, "corporations are increasingly pumping money into grassroots sports organizations, and, in turn, grassroots sports organizations are better able to provide corporations with substantial returns on their investments" (p. 42). These companies are realizing that speaking to consumers in a local environment may be more persuasive than through nationwide involvement.

One of the issues surrounding grassroots sport sponsorship is related to the professionalism of the local organization. This concern seems logical since national corporations tend to be less secure about putting their brand image in the hands of volunteers or unproven local organizers than they would be with major sport organizations or professional leagues. One industry executive commented, "There are just too many bad events. An event might have a couple of thousand kids, but not the media and PR. You pay a guy a couple of thousand dollars to support an event and you never know what happened" (Joyce, 2003, p. 8). On a related note, it could also hold true that the nature of the sponsor could influence the audience's perception of the event. If the sponsor is held in high regard by the audience, the event may also benefit from that positive attitude.

The quest for sponsors can be an exciting and rewarding one, but be assured that the sport marketer must consider the needs and objectives of the sponsor. The marketing director for Anaheim Sports cautioned sport administrators to avoid sponsor relationships that can evolve into situations in which the sponsors desire more for their money than has previously been delivered. He said, "We can't just put their sign up but must figure out how to drive traffic in their store or service" (Goldberg, 1998b, p. 29). Sponsorship consultant Kim Skildum-Reid (2012) commented that "flashing your logo in front of masses of cynical consumers does not equal marketing return" (p. 4). The collective criteria used by sponsors to evaluate sponsorship opportunities do not seem to vary considerably from one company to another. However, each corporation, depending on its marketing strategy and current market position, values certain criteria differently. Therefore, sport marketers attempting to develop sponsorship proposals must understand the criteria and tailor proposals to specific sponsors.

Best Practice — FedEx's Sponsorship Recipe

With equal parts of local and national events with indirect revenue, FedEx has developed a portfolio framework that is integrated, actionable, measurable, and represents best practice in the field.

The portfolio is segmented by objective, not price. Internal teams are divided into two complementary camps, not one. And sponsorships as a tactical discipline are used in no fewer than five very different ways. Other brands focus on businesses [b-to-b] or consumers [b-to-c], but FedEx has to keep both on the radar screen. Although the primary target is in the b-to-b world, the company must build its umbrella name inside the b-to-c universe to ensure one of the most ubiquitous brands maintains its leadership status. "We are constantly reminding ourselves that we are not merely in the business of sponsoring things," said managing director of sponsorships Kevin Demsky. "We are in the business of convincing customers to utilize our services. Sponsorships are just a conduit to accomplishing the corporate objective."

That conduit plays a pivotal role inside the marketing machine, as evidenced by the business FedEx signs at events, the revenue generated direct from properties, and the strategic way the company uses sponsorships to invade new markets and maintain presence in existing operating regions. Using sponsorships, [FedEx has] penetrated new areas and grown share faster than we could have before. They create an anchor point in the marketing mix.

FedEx has eight rules for winning the game of sponsorships:

1. Sponsorships Are Not Created Equal

   There are five corporate goals for sponsorships: Drive revenue; provide an opportunity to entertain customers in a unique environment; give sales a platform for developing relationships; create benefits for employees; and drive the brand.

   FedEx marketers realize few sponsorships can score five-for-five. "We recognize that not all properties can deliver on all goals," Demsky said. Different sponsorships deliver on different objectives, and only when marketers acknowledge that can they develop a portfolio in which a series of properties achieve goals together. FedEx builds a "collection" of sponsorships that together helps move the needle.

2. Structure Portfolios by Objective, Not Price

   If sponsorships are not created equal and can only achieve some of the five objectives, properties must be segmented into a portfolio that plays to the strengths and challenges of each. According to FedEx, "Sponsorships deliver different benefits, so we've built a unique framework that allows us to see how our properties contribute," Demsky said. It's a strategic framework for defining the different pieces of the portfolio in a way that allows the company to analyze and make decisions on performance. FedEx uses a five-tier portfolio structure to categorize sponsorships by objective instead of by price (see below).

   Category 5: Hospitality Events. Sponsorships should create "focused, private, extended" windows in which to invite customers to interact with FedEx. Such events are used to build relationships and learn more about prospects' businesses.

   Category 4: Hometown Events. Through acquisition, FedEx's home is no longer solely in Memphis. For example, FedEx Ground is based in Pittsburgh and FedEx Custom Critical operates in Akron, OH. Category 4 sponsorships keep the brand visible in the communities where it affects economic and social areas.

Category 3: Key Targets. This category was put in place to affect a specific geographic region or a specific demographic target. "For example, if our local marketing teams decide they need to penetrate Denver, my group will go out and set up a robust sponsorship plan to help drive business in that region," Demsky said.

Category 2: Revenue and Supply Chain Events. FedEx partners with properties that integrate the company's services into its own operations. The integration is then used as a compelling case study to share with customers and prospects about how FedEx helps businesses run more smoothly. Direct revenue is a secondary benefit for the property buying FedEx's services.

Category 1: Leadership Events. The crown jewels leveraged across multiple channels and used on a national basis achieve most of the five corporate goals. "We can do a little bit of everything with these events," Demsky said. "This is the one category that, because we can do so many things, we invest in a variety of activation vehicles."

In a system based on objectives, size doesn't matter. A FedEx Forum sits in Category 4, an NFL in Category 1, and FedEx Field, used to incorporate FedEx into the critical Washington, DC market, in Category 3. "The structure allows us to tailor our investments," said VP of marketing Brian Phillips. "Each property comes with a different set of expectations, and we calibrate our ROI calculation based on the category."

3. Measure Independently

An organization that treats every sponsorship independently needs an ROI system that measures each property singularly.

The company is getting ready to come out of the closet with an Index Measurement Tool that will calculate specific ratings based on property performance. "If we have a category model that recognizes no two sponsorships are the same, then we need a tool that will give us an accurate barometer to see if events are doing what we expect them to do," Demsky said.

The tool involves an "objective template" that is laid on top of sponsorships to generate a score that indicates whether or not an event is performing. The different scores are then combined to gauge the performance of the overall portfolio. "We don't expect a FedEx Field to have the same ROI as a PGA, so the Index Tool will help normalize the differences between properties and help us measure events on equal footing," Demsky said.

If a property scores poorly, FedEx will meet with the partner and try to identify ways to raise the number. If the score still remains low, it's an indication that the property may be ready for elimination from the portfolio.

4. Pass On Awareness

If a property primarily represents impressions, FedEx takes a pass—quickly. After all, with recognition near 100 percent, eyeballs are appreciated but not necessary.

"Certainly, awareness is something that we are interested in creating, but only if it's a byproduct of a sponsorship," Demsky said. "In the hierarchy of benefits that come from sponsorship investments, it's not high on our list of must-haves."

More important are elements that push leads, anchor the brand, and provide face time. Impressions end up as icing on the sponsorship cake. "This company is measured by how many packages are shipped, and our sponsorships are measured by their contribution in driving those shipments," Demsky said. "It's too easy to get focused on how many eyeballs saw the brand that you lose focus on how many of those eyeballs pulled out their wallets."

5. Sponsorships 'Plus-Up' the Mix

Smart marketers integrate sponsorships throughout the marketing mix, not the other way around. "Certainly, advertising, direct-response, and promotions are important on their own, but sponsorships provide a healthy way to plus-up the marketing mix beyond the events," said David Grant, a principal with longtime FedEx event agency Velocity Sports and Entertainment, Wilton, Connecticut. "Sponsorship is a tool in and of itself, but it's also a tool to make everything else a little bit better. We're now using sponsorships as a more strategic tool and recognizing that we can integrate our events throughout the entire mix."

6. A House with Two Sides

Without a solid internal structure, sponsorships can't be identified, managed, or serviced. Keep it simple and focused by creating two sides to the sponsorship team, one that manages the present and another that focuses on the future. FedEx has a core team of 11 in-house members in its event department. One of the teams is focused on activating and leveraging investments already made via marketing programs, promotional components, hospitality efforts, and so on. On the other side of the house is another team responsible for managing the growth of the portfolio. They identify new sponsorship opportunities, decide whether or not the portfolio has the right mix, and oversee all selection, planning, and negotiations. Each team has staffers attached to specific properties. They manage all aspects of the deals, working with rights-holders, as well as other FedEx business units that may leverage the sponsorships.

7. Make Hospitality a Marketing Extension

Hospitality elements provide a platform for live extensions of branding. A sport organization's tagline, images, thematics, and attributes should come alive on-site. FedEx ties hospitality to different umbrella marketing messages. The Super Bowl annually sports hospitality interactives tied to the Air and Ground offerings. PGA events are used to showcase FedEx's reliability. At Gillette Stadium, the company brought its new "Relax. It's FedEx" tagline to life with a Relax Zone boasting soothing music, candles, and massages.

Hospitality must also be immersive. At the St. Jude Classic, for instance, FedEx erects a two-story structure that rivals any golf clubhouse. It's less about food and drinks, and more about isolated environments for building relationships. "We've learned the average company employee doesn't have the authority to choose which company their employer uses to ship a package," Demsky said. "And for those individuals that do have the authority, it's a complicated decision. So in order to help our salespeople get some time with those customers, we create the quality time in which to have a discussion."

FedEx also makes the most of hospitality with off-hour events for customers and prospects. Last winter, for example, the company created NFL Open Houses in five markets in which as many as 500 customers were brought in on an off-day for activities, entertainment, behind-the-scenes tours, and chalk talks with players. The hospitality blueprint follows no fewer than six points of communication with the target called pre-invite, formal "save the date" invitation, a "what to expect" message, itinerary, the on-site event, and a follow-up.

8. Say When

There's nothing wrong with window-shopping, but event marketers should know when the portfolio has had enough. "If you have 20 properties that you need to actively leverage, you have too many properties," Grant said. If the return is not meeting objectives, then it may be more of an issue in which property is not delivering rather than in which property needs to be added.

Cover Story: *Game On*. (2004, May 4). Event Marketer. Retrieved from www.eventmarketer.com/viewMedia.asp?prmMID=511. Reprinted with permission.

Recommended Additional Reading

Motion, J., Leitch, S., & Brodie, R. (2003). Equity in corporate co-branding. *European Journal of Marketing, 37*(7/8), 1080–1094.

Skildum-Reid, K. (2012). The corporate sponsorship toolkit. Sydney, Australia: Freya Press.

Sponsor Needs Worksheets

The worksheets guide the development of various sections of your sponsorship plan. The following sheets cover sponsor needs and rationale. Complete this worksheet as you would prepare a sponsorship plan.

Identify the demographics of your team event and match them to those of your potential sponsor.

_____

_____

_____

_____

_____

_____

_____

_____

_____

Determine the psychographic and image match between the sponsor's product and your property.

_____

_____

_____

_____

_____

_____

_____

_____

_____

Enumerate possible awareness objectives that could be accomplished through the sponsorship.

_____

_____

_____

_____

_____

_____

_____

_____

_____

Cite possible image objectives that could be accomplished through the sponsorship.

_____

_____

_____

_____

_____

_____

_____

_____

Itemize possible sales objectives that could be accomplished through the sponsorship.

_____
_____
_____
_____
_____
_____
_____
_____
_____
_____

Describe possible hospitality objectives that could be accomplished through the sponsorship.

_____
_____
_____
_____
_____
_____
_____
_____
_____
_____

Present possible employee motivation objectives that could be accomplished through the sponsorship.

_____
_____
_____
_____
_____
_____
_____
_____
_____
_____

Determine and describe the potential for on-site sales and whole-saler tie-ins that could be accomplished through the sponsorship.

_____
_____
_____
_____
_____

_____
_____
_____

Discuss the potential for cross-promotions that could be possible through the sponsorship.

_____
_____
_____
_____
_____
_____
_____
_____

Consider potential issues in integrated communications regarding the timing of the sponsorship and the sponsor's business activities.

_____
_____
_____
_____
_____
_____
_____
_____

List all current sponsors and reflect on any conflicts that may surface.

_____
_____
_____
_____
_____
_____
_____
_____

Detail the nature of cooperation obtained from the venue/facility.

_____
_____

_____

_____

_____

_____

_____

Outline any conceivable risks that may result from the sponsorship.

_____

_____

_____

_____

_____

_____

_____

_____

Discuss the potential of all cause-related sponsorship options.

_____

_____

_____

_____

_____

_____

_____

Determine if any grassroots sponsorship options may be available for sponsors.

_____

_____

_____

_____

_____

_____

_____

4

Olympic Sponsorship Opportunities

THE OLYMPIC MOVEMENT AND SPONSORSHIP

Olympic and amateur sport organizations, throughout the past Olympiads, have come increasingly to depend on corporate sponsors who have supplied much-needed revenue in difficult financial times. The dependency of the Olympic movement on corporate sponsors is evidenced by the statistic showing that over 30% of the International Olympic Committee's budget and about 40% of the United States Olympic Committee's (USOC) funds are derived from sponsorship and licensing income ("Financial," n.d.; Olympic Fact File, 2012). Specifically, for the period ending in 2011, the USOC had revenues totaling $1.2 billion with income from its sponsorship program at $75.4 million, and royalty and rights fees totaling $75.4 million and $2.6 million respectively ("Financial," n.d.). Olympic Organizing Committees also increasingly depend on these resources. Sponsorship revenue for the London 2012 Olympic Games accounted for 54% of all income (Cutler, 2012; Olympic Fact File, 2012). Reports for the 2010 Winter Olympic Games showed that 42% of the Vancouver Organizing Committee (VANOC) revenues were derived from sponsorships (International Olympic Committee, 2012).

One aspect of the Olympic movement that has attracted sponsors is the global power represented in the Olympic symbol, the five interlocking rings. The Olympic Rings have shown to be the most recognizable logo in the world with 89.8% of the population capable of correctly recognizing the symbol (Olympic Fact File, 2012). Thus, associating with the Olympic Rings would be highly prized by leading corporations and could increase corporate exposure to the cumulative worldwide television audience of 4.8 billion viewers who typically watch the Games either in person or through the global television coverage (Olympic Fact File, 2012).

Sponsorship and the Olympic Games have existed since the Games' inception. In ancient Greece, city-states and merchants supported many athletes. With the revival of the Games in 1896, Kodak placed an ad in the official program of the first modern Olympics. Although Kodak dropped out as an Olympic sponsor in 2008, it was the longest standing Olympic Sponsor. That title now belongs to Coca-Cola. It was in 1928 that

Coca-Cola began its long-standing relationship with the Olympic movement (Olympic Fact File, 2012). Sponsorship and the Olympics have a well-established relationship and one that has significantly increased in complexity.

COMMERCIALIZATION OF THE OLYMPIC GAMES

The sport industry witnessed a transition between the 1976 Montreal Olympic Games and the 1984 Los Angeles Games. Currently, most people are aware of the intense financial burden the 1976 Games placed on Montreal, more than a $1-billion debt, and of the overt commercialization of the 1984 Games, as well. Through its efforts to attract corporate sponsors, the Los Angeles Olympic Organizing Committee was able to operate the Games and generate a profit in excess of $225 million. "There [were] plenty of opportunities for sale in the five-ring circus: television, commercials, product licensing, product exclusivity at the Games, team sponsorships, Olympic movement sponsorships, awards presentations, training center support, product endorsements, and almost anything a marketing [person] could devise" (Marsano, 1987, p. 65). Since the commercialization in 1984 and the realization of substantial profits, sponsorship has become an integral part of the Olympic movement.

Corporate rationale for Olympic sponsorship is quite similar to the rationale for other sponsorship activities. Carter and Wilkinson (2002) explored sponsor rationale for the 2000 Sydney Games. They found that the top ranked objective was increasing brand awareness, followed by reaching an appropriate audience, showcasing products, and increasing employee morale. Results from their study showed that hospitality objectives were ranked somewhat lower than in other studies. It is important to note that there was significant variance between these factors and the level of sponsorship, which demonstrated that different sponsors sought different objectives. Furthermore, Carter and Wilkinson's research (2002) indicates that high levels of variance also exist between sponsoring companies.

OLYMPIC SPONSORSHIP RIGHTS AND PRIVILEGES

There are five different types of Olympic sponsorships in which corporations could become involved: *national governing bodies*, *national Olympic committees*, *Olympic organizing committees*, the IOC's worldwide *Olympic sponsorship program*, and the *International Olympic Committee* itself. Each entity provides specific sponsor rights associated with participation.

National Governing Bodies

At the base of the Olympic organization, the national governing bodies (NGBs) have engaged in a variety of sponsorship activities. Each Olympic sport has an NGB in each country that is a member of the IOC. These organizations can grant sponsorship rights to companies for activities for their sport within a single country. It is important to understand that sponsors of NGBs can gain access to the team members of that sport, the uniforms of that sport, and the NGB's logo but not the Olympic Rings. U.S. Skiing has successfully managed its sponsorship programs for many years, independently from the

USOC. Audi signed a sponsorship agreement as Official Automotive Sponsor of the U.S. Ski Team. Audi's chief marketing officer commented that "the U.S. ski team is a globally recognized symbol of peak performance and precision, making it a perfect fit with Audi's Quattro all-wheel drive system and Audi's world-renowned luxury vehicles" (Audi of America, 2007, p. 3).

USA Gymnastics continues to work with Olympic sponsor Visa. The two signed an agreement for Visa to be the title sponsor of the USA Gymnastics Championships, to be called the Visa Championships. Through the sponsorship, Visa also becomes the official payment sponsor. USA Gymnastics President Bob Colarossi said, "VISA has been a valuable contributor and marketing partner for the organization and we look forward to another successful Olympic quadrennium together as we jointly develop programs for the Olympic Games" (Eaton, 2004, p. 9).

The U.S. Soccer Federation recently signed Nike to a 10-year sponsorship worth $120 million. Their agreement stipulates that Nike will support youth development programs and provide equipment and uniforms to all U.S. national teams. Nike also secured deals with soccer governing bodies in several other nations, which included some of the world's top teams, the Netherlands, Brazil, Nigeria, and South Korea.

Several successful NGB sponsorship arrangements were consummated for the Athens Olympic Games. Nautica International signed up as the official apparel supplier for U.S. Sailing, and through the arrangement Nautica supplied outfits for the 130 members of the U.S. Sailing Team, the U.S. Disabled Sailing Team, and the U.S. Sailing World Youth Team ("Nautica Signs," 2004).

National Olympic Committees

A national Olympic committee (NOC) can authorize the use of the Olympic rings but only in conjunction with its respective logo. For the United States Olympic Committee (USOC), that would mean using the designated symbols of the USOC as defined in its graphic standards manual. The new-for-2012 USOC symbol depicts the Olympic Rings accompanied by the American flag.

Any USOC logo must, of course, adhere to the rigorous specifications outlined by the USOC. For the quadrennium ending in 2012, the USOC secured sponsorships at the Partner level (approx. $35 million each), the highest level offered by the USOC, with AT&T, Anheuser-Busch, United Airlines, Citi Group, and BMW. All domestic partners, sponsors, and suppliers receive marketing rights to the U.S. Olympic Team and commercial access to Olympic themes, terminology, and imagery for use in sponsor marketing and advertising programs. These sponsors would have the right to proclaim themselves USOC sponsors and sponsors of the U.S. Olympic Team. For example, Nike secured the rights through 2020 as the Official Outfitter of the U.S. Olympic Team, "allowing" (or *requiring*) athletes to showcase Nike products on the medals podium at the Olympic Games. Clothier Ralph Lauren signed in 2008 as the provider of apparel for the opening and closing ceremonies of the Beijing and London Olympic Games. One controversy arose for both Nike and Ralph Lauren when it was discovered that the 2012 outfits for the Team USA were made in China. The companies pledged to guarantee that outfits for all future U.S. Olympic teams would be made in the USA. Both sponsors have renewed through 2020.

According to the USOC, "the 'Sponsor' level (approx. $15 million each) represents the level of corporate support required to gain access to the USOC logo as an 'Official Sponsor' and commercial access to Olympic themes, terminology, and imagery for use in sponsor marketing programs" (Giannoulakis, Stotlar, & Chatziefstathiou, 2008, p. 259). USOC Sponsors provide significant levels of cash, products, or services in support of the U.S. Olympic Team and may also choose to extend their U.S. Olympic investment to include National NGBs, the U.S. Paralympic Team, and/or U.S. Olympic Signature Property events and programs. Sponsors at this level include such companies as All State Insurance, Kellogg, 24 Hour Fitness and All State Insurance, among others. An array of other companies has bought in at the Supplier level (approximately $3–10 million each), which provides access only to the USOC Supplier logo that also includes the rings. All domestic partners, sponsors, and suppliers receive marketing rights to the U.S. Olympic Team and conduct all advertising and marketing programs within the U.S.

Because the 2002 Olympic Games were held in the United States (Salt Lake City), the USOC developed a new marketing and sponsorship program in 1998 entitled Olympic Properties of the United States (OPUS). This program was designed with constructs similar to those of the ACOP program administered for the 1996 Atlanta Games. This program provided access to the benefits offered by the USOC together with properties associated with the Salt Lake Organizing Committee. One of the new sponsors signed up by OPUS was General Motors. The $1 billion, eight-year deal allowed GM to market a variety of vehicles to the diverse audience that the Olympic Games represented and to introduce new models in conjunction with the launch of each Olympic Games during the contract period (Rozin, 1998).

Interestingly, Olympic training centers around the U.S. are responsible for securing their own sponsorship arrangements. However, in most cases, they work very closely with the USOC marketing and sponsorship division. Many of the Olympic Training Center agreements encompass in-kind donations of products and services.

Olympic Organizing Committees

The Olympic organizing committees (OOCs) have also benefited from both television revenues and from sponsorship agreements. Worldwide television revenues for the 2012 London Olympic Games were estimated at $8 billion (yes, billion). In 2004, the formula for allocation of Olympic television rights changed such that the funds would be shared on the basis of 49% to the OOC and 51% to the Olympic movement. The breakdown specifies that the IOC share revenues with the international federations (IFs) for the Summer and Winter sports. Beginning in 2006, the Winter IFs received 33.3% of the funds, and the Summer Games IFs got 66.6%. A review of the TV rights fees paid by U.S. broadcasting companies has been provided at the conclusion of this chapter in Table 4.1. As noted earlier, as much as 50% of an organizing committee's budget may be generated through sponsorships. The rights involved with an organizing committee may include official suppliers, sponsors, and licensing agreements. The 2012 London Games brought in $8 billion from its partnerships (International Olympic Committee, 2012; Murray, 2012).

The organizing committee is able to reduce budget demands through the value-in-kind (VIK) supplies, and the sponsor is able to associate its products/services with the Games. Some of the more traditional examples include the sponsorship of awards, transportation, communication systems, and various sport-specific equipment. In 2012, London was able to secure sponsorship from adidas for Games apparel, Lloyd's TSB for financial services, and BMW for official vehicles. Interestingly, BMW paid over $100 million for these rights while adidas paid $80 million, both higher than fees paid by the IOC's Worldwide Olympic sponsors. Adidas was able to recoup a significant portion of its sponsorship fee by selling $156 million in London 2012-licensed merchandise. The price for a national sponsorship at the 2016 Rio Games has been estimated at $300 million. It seems that access to open categories has value. Ventures such as these have been very popular with both organizing committees and sponsors.

The Olympic Partners

In 1985, the IOC created a program to make the world's most complicated sport marketing purchase a one-stop shopping venture for international corporations (Marsano, 1987, p. 65). No longer would companies endure the trauma of multiple negotiations that often produced only narrow results. What ensued was known as "The Olympic Programme," now entitled The Olympic Partners (TOP). The first TOP program covered 1985 to 1988, while TOP II provided sponsors with benefits from 1989 to 1992, and TOP III regulated sponsor activity from 1990 to 1996. Similarly, TOP IV's time frame included the 1998 Nagano Olympics and the 2000 Olympic Games in Sydney. TOP V covered the Winter Games of 2002 in Salt Lake City and the 2004 Summer Games in Athens, while the TOP VI program included Torino and Beijing. Eleven sponsors signed up for TOP VII covering Vancouver and London (Olympic Fact File, 2012).

The system was patterned after the success of the Los Angeles Games, which demonstrated that having fewer sponsors who paid more money was better for organizers and sponsors alike. TOP established a system whereby a limited number of sponsors would receive special treatment and benefits on a worldwide basis while achieving product category exclusivity and protection for their Olympic sponsorship activities. Specifically, TOP sponsors receive the following benefits (International Olympic Committee, 2004):

1. Product Exclusivity: Only one sponsor is allowed for any product category. This means that as long as Coca-Cola and Visa are members of the TOP, then Pepsi and American Express will not be allowed to become involved with Olympic sponsorship on any level, international, national, or with the organizing committee.

2. Use of Olympic Marks, Imagery, and Designations: Each participant is granted the right to use the solitary Olympic rings, as well as the use of the rings in combination with all 202 NOC designations. This provides both worldwide and local

impact. Companies can also use the "Official Sponsor" and "Official Product" designations for all Organizing Committees in addition to the OOC logos.

3. Public Relations and Promotional Opportunities: Sponsors are given special tie-ins and media events to increase their exposure.

4. Access to Olympic Archives: The IOC makes available articles, photographs, and video footage from the Olympic museum and archives in Switzerland to sponsors for special exhibits and displays.

5. Olympic Merchandise and Premiums: Clothing and apparel bearing the Olympic logos can be used for sales incentives and marketing activities organized by each sponsor.

6. Tickets and Hospitality: Sponsors receive priority access to seating at both the Winter and Summer Games.

7. Advertising Options: Each participant in TOP is given first chance at souvenir program ads and the right of first refusal in purchasing advertising on Olympic broadcasts.

8. On-site Participation: Point-of-purchase and product display are included in the package. Companies gain certain rights to concession areas and space for product sampling. Showcase opportunities are also made available on the Olympic venue grounds.

9. Research: Each sponsor receives a full research report on the public's reception of his/her participation and an assessment of the value-added benefits.

10. First Right of Negotiation for the Next Quadrennial: All worldwide sponsors with TOP have the option to continue in their product category.

The nine initial clients in the TOP I program contributed a total of $95 million in revenues. For sponsors, TOP I proved to be a resounding success in 1988. Subsequently, the program produced $175 million for TOP II, $350 million for TOP III, and $500 million for TOP IV, ending with the Sydney Games (TOP IV Programme, 1997). The TOP V program, which covered the 2002 Winter Games in Salt Lake City and the 2004 Summer Games in Athens, generated $663 million, while the TOP VI program of Torino and Beijing generated $866 million in revenues. The eleven companies in the Vancouver-London TOP VII program accounted for $957 million in revenues (Olympic Fact File, 2012). TOP VII companies and their representative categories, through the London and Vancouver Olympic Games (Olympic Fact File, 2012):

Company	Category
Coca-Cola	Nonalcoholic beverage
Atos Origin	Information technology
Dow Chemical	Official chemical company
Proctor and Gamble	Personal care and household products
Visa	Consumer payment systems
Panasonic-Matsushita	Television/video/audio equipment
Samsung	Wireless communications equipment

McDonald's . . . . Retail food services
General Electric . . . . Various equipment and services
Omega . . . . Timing, scoring and venue results
Acer . . . . Computing technology/equipment

Kodak was actually an advertiser in the program for the first Olympics of the modern era in 1896, and Coca-Cola became a supplier for the Olympics in 1928. Omega had on-and-off engagements in official timing for various Games. Each set of Games recruited suppliers and other supporters over the years, but not until 1986 when the TOP program was initiated did the program really take shape. Coca-Cola, Visa, and Panasonic are the lone remaining members of TOP I. Samsung and McDonald's signed up as members of the TOP IV program in 1997. The arrangement with Samsung provided the 1998 and 2000 Games with wireless communications equipment. This asset was deemed to be "vital to the achievement of a smooth and successful running of the Games" ("Two New Partners," 1997, p. 9). In addition, they provided over 20,000 cellular telephones to officials and participating teams. Another unique service is their "Rendezvous at Samsung" program, which allow athletes to contact their families immediately after their events in a media-proof and comfortable setting. Samsung's Group President said that the Olympic spirit of world peace and contribution to society is at one with Samsung's ideals. McDonald's decided to expand its 1996 sponsorship activities in Atlanta's Olympic Village and, over the ensuing years, has become a worldwide partner by activating its sponsorship not only at the Games but in its restaurants in the 202 countries involved in the Games. Beginning in 2008 for the Beijing Olympics, the McDonald's Olympic Champion Crew program recognized and rewarded 1,400 of its best-of-the-best restaurant employees from around the world with travel to Beijing to serve the world's best athletes and thousands of others at McDonald's four new Olympic venue restaurants.

For McDonald's, the rationale was customer oriented: Now all of our customers around the world can share in the fun and excitement of the Olympic Games (Olympic Fact File, 2012). McDonald's leveraged its Worldwide Partner status with the Canadian Olympic Committee by supporting Olympic School Day runs across Canada prior to the Games. Other global activities included a European program called "Go Active" featuring the promotion of adult happy meals that included a salad, water, and free stepometer. In China, they featured cups with Olympic athletes, and in Japan, they ran an Olympic-themed game with instant-win coupons and premium prizes. Proctor & Gamble promoted its Olympic sponsorship through the "Proud of Moms" theme. Proctor & Gamble's Olympics Project Director claimed that concerning impact of the company's sponsorship of the London Games, "one of the things we [P&G] have always struggled with is to find a big enough commercial and marketing platform we could leverage. No one knows who P&G are, but I always tell people what we own. London Games gave P&G a platform and that resulted in more integration within the company as the Games had involved all departments at P&G, not just marketing. As a result, the Games sky-rocketed the P&G brand in the minds of consumers" ("Olympic Sponsorship," 2012, para. 1). It was, in fact, found to be the most effective of all 2012 Olympic Sponsorship programs, increasing P&G favorability by 10% and producing more than $100 million in incremental sales ("Olympic Sponsorship," 2012).

A relatively new benefit for TOP Sponsors is the IOC's Youth Olympic Games. Begun in Singapore (Summer, 2010) and continuing to Innsbruck (Winter, 2012), the Youth Olympic Games offers TOP sponsors the opportunity to start brand preference strategies at a very early age.

Financials

The disbursement policy provides that revenues derived from the TOP program must be shared. The proportion of revenues allocated to the various Olympic entities is as follows ("Greater TOP Support," 1999; International Olympic Committee, 2012; Michel, 1991):

- 40% of the funds are allotted to the participating national Olympic committees. The precise distribution is based on a formula whereby the money is divided with each NOC* receiving a set dollar amount (minimum of $40,000) plus an additional amount per athlete qualifying for the Games.
- 50% of the TOP funds are disbursed to the participating Olympic organizing committees. Within these parameters, the Winter Games organizing committee receives 10% of the total monies while the Summer Games organizing committee is allotted 40%.
- The IOC keeps the remaining 10% (International Olympic Committee, 2012).

The corporations involved in TOP have a significant involvement in the Games and present myriad justifications and explanations for their participation. The Olympic Games present a variety of opportunities for Coke. They continue to sponsor the Olympic Torch Relay and the popular on-site Olympic Pin Trading Centre. To promote its products, Coke supplies the Olympic Village (athletes) with no-charge vending machines and has exclusive pouring rights for beverages at Olympic venues. Coke's Board of Directors Chair commented, "As a global company, we feel it is important for us to be a part of such a powerful movement" (International Olympic Committee, 1998, p. 51).

Olympic sponsorship has been of immense benefit to the Visa brand and overall image. As noted in Chapter 9, Visa has gained substantial market share through its Olympic involvement and has been very successful through advertising, which highlights its exclusive vendor position with Olympic ticket sales. As a part of its TOP program, it has established special Visa NET systems to link thousands of ATMs in over 200 countries. It has also supported a variety of the cultural and educational exhibits during the Games. The benefit of Olympic sponsorship for Visa was activating a "powerful tool to help us achieve our objectives of building the Visa brand and providing our members

---

* Since TOP's inception 20 years ago, the USOC has received 20% of all TOP funds and 12.75% of NBC's broadcast fees. The original leverage was based on the high proportion of sponsors originating from U.S. companies and NBC broadcast money. U.S. sources currently account for 62% of revenues. Since 2008, many IOC members called for a revision of this revenue-sharing formula. After the 2012 London Games, new formulas were agreed upon in principle.

and merchants with opportunities to build their business. No single sponsorship property has delivered stronger returns for our members and merchants than the Olympic Games" ("Visa USA," 2004, p. 2).

The Olympic Games provide an opportunity for Panasonic to showcase its technology as the principal contractor for the Olympic Broadcast Centre (OBC). The OBC is the facility from which all television signals emanate. In addition to the OBC, Panasonic provides more than 20 giant screens and video-on-demand units at various locations in the Olympic host city. Panasonic's rationale centers on having its corporate name associated with this premier international athletic event (International Olympic Committee, 2012). Furthermore, General Electric has used its sponsorship to demonstrate its technological capabilities across a variety of industries, from broadcast (e.g., NBC) to medical technology (e.g., MRI) used in the Olympic medical centers. GE was also able to secure over $300 million in wind turbine business across China after the 2008 Games due in part to its relationship with government officials in Beijing.

TOP has served two major goals of the Olympic movement. It has made the IOC less dependent on television revenues, and it has assisted all countries in the world with sport development through a shared revenue system.

PARALYMPICS

Another Olympic-related event is the Paralympic Games. The Summer and Winter Paralympic events follow the regularly scheduled Olympic Games by two weeks and provide competition for the world's elite athletes with disabilities. This differs appreciably from the Special Olympics, which provides opportunities for mentally disabled participants. The Paralympics have been extremely successful in showcasing the talents of elite athletes with disabilities, such as blindness, amputation, or paralysis and has grown significantly since the first Paralympics were held in 1960 in Rome, Italy, where 400 athletes from 23 countries participated. The London 2012 Summer Paralympic Games featured 4,200 athletes from 165 countries ("It's Official," 2012). The mission of the U.S. Olympians and Paralympians Association is "to create and implement programs that will integrate Olympians & Paralympians into every facet of the Olympic Movement. In support of the goals of the United States Olympic Committee, U.S. Olympians & Paralympians strive to foster the spirit of Olympism in each community, to motivate and encourage youth and to develop camaraderie among those who have shared the unique experience of representing their nation at the Olympic & Paralympic Games" (U.S. Paralympics, n.d., para. 1).

As an affiliate of the USOC, ties with USOC sponsors are strong; however, the U.S. Paralympic organization has the right to pursue sponsorship independently. In 2004, just prior to the Athens Olympics, the U.S. Paralympic team secured a sponsorship from Chrysler as its official vehicle sponsor. Chrysler worked with Olympic Gold Medalist Chris Waddell to reach out to rehabilitation hospitals across the U.S. through a multiple city tour. Similarly, former TOP sponsor John Hancock allowed U.S. Paralympics to pursue and secure The Hartford as its insurance sponsor, based in part on The Hartford's long-time association with disabled sport.

Ralph Lauren, Nike, and many of the other sponsors of the USOC contribute to the U.S. Paralympic team. The division of funds between the USOC and Paralympics is handled internally, but the support is significant to the U.S. Paralympic team's success. The USOC provides other funding for the U.S. Paralympic team, but the funding provided for Paralympic athletes is substantially less than that provided for the able-bodied Olympic athletes and increases the need of the organization to seek sponsors independently.

AMBUSH MARKETING

As the cost of obtaining sponsorship rights with sport organizations began to escalate, some companies started to explore methods that could deliver the same impact as a sport sponsorship but at a reduced cost. Some corporate marketers decided they would attempt to associate their company with sport events without paying the requisite sponsorship fee. This tactic soon became known as *ambush marketing*. Ambush marketing has been defined as "a promotional strategy whereby a non-sponsor attempts to capitalize on the popularity/prestige of a property by giving the false impression that it is a sponsor. [This tactic is] often employed by the competitors of a property's official sponsors" (Ukman, 1995b, p. 42). Several prominent examples of ambush marketing have developed within the sport industry and it appears that the practice is still growing.

Significant debate surrounds the practice of ambush marketing. Skildum-Reid noted that everyone has an opinion. "It's stealing, it's clever, it's guerrilla marketing; when it happens, the topic always turns to ethics. Is it right or is it wrong?" (Skildum-Reid, 2007, p. xii).

The modern history of ambush marketing in sport started at the 1984 Olympic Games when Kodak cleverly ambushed Fuji Film. Although Fuji had purchased the right to be an official sponsor from the Los Angeles Olympic Organizing Committee, the public was convinced that Kodak, not Fuji, was the official sponsor (Hotzau, 2007). By purchasing sponsorships with the USOC and buying numerous television ads during the Games, Kodak created the perception that they were an official sponsor of the Olympic Games. Kodak did not mislead the public but merely leveraged the public's ignorance about the newly conceived Olympic sponsorship concept.

In some instances, the Olympic organizers are partially to blame for allowing ambush marketing activities. In an effort to commemorate the Games, the Los Angeles City Council approved a name-change for one of its thoroughfares to "Olympic Boulevard." As a result, hundreds of businesses relocated to the street and opened up with names like Olympic Cleaners and Olympic Limousines. These measures were deemed to be legal because businesses were allowed, under city statute, to use their street location name as part of their business identity.

Nike cleverly had murals painted on the sides of assorted downtown Los Angeles buildings during the 1984 Games (Myerson, 1996). The same strategy was averted for 1996 in Atlanta when the City Council passed a ban on large-scale outdoor advertising. Reebok officials unsuccessfully argued that its proposed 60-by-80-foot mural of Shaquille O'Neal was public art. However, several companies discovered a loophole since the regulations did not include large portable signage or building-sized projected images (Bayor, 1996).

Nike was an active ambush marketer during the 2012 London Olympic Games. Their ad campaign was titled "Find Your Greatness." Their TV ads featured athletes all over the world in towns and cities named London (Ontario, Canada; Nigeria, etc.). Nike also leveraged their sponsorship with USA Soccer with specially designed T-shirts donned by U.S. women's team members after their Gold medal game.

American Express and Visa have had continuous battles over legitimate sponsorship rights and alleged ambush tactics since 1988. Visa aired advertising that claimed that the Olympics would not take American Express cards. This was technically accurate in reference to the official ticket outlets. However, various tour companies and other travel-related services would accept American Express cards in payment. During the 1992 Barcelona Games, American Express constructed its own advertising campaign claiming that you did not need a visa, as opposed to Visa card, to go to Barcelona (Hotzau, 2007). Note that no mention was made of the Olympic Games. As a final ploy in its strategy, American Express purchased sponsorship rights to the hotel key fobs at the IOC headquarters hotel in Barcelona. The key fobs were shaped and colored like an American Express card on one side and had hotel information on the other.

Ambush marketing tactics are not confined to overzealous corporations. The City of Atlanta Convention and Visitors Bureau tried to sell sponsorships during the 1996 Games in conflict with the Atlanta Olympic Organizing Committee program. They were, however, bought-off by the organizing committee for $3 million (Hotzau, 2007). Former IOC Vice President Dick Pound commented, "It never occurred to anybody that a city would ever think of ambushing its own organizing committee" (Wells, 1996, p. 53). The IOC was so concerned about some citizens believing ambush marketing was clever or inspired that they began using the term *parasite marketing* to convey a less-than-positive impression of the practice. Protection against this type of ambush is now required in the bid documents submitted for consideration in hosting the Games.

For London 2012, legislation prohibited the use of the words Olympic, Games, 2012, twenty-twelve, in any combination with London, summer, sponsor, medals, summer, gold, silver, bronze. Of course, any use of the Olympic five rings, or any facsimile thereof, was also prohibited. Any infringement of the rules would first be dealt with through an order for cessation followed by confiscation and destruction of goods. Furthermore, the offender would be required to forfeit all profits and could be fined up to five times the estimated profits.

During the London 2012 Olympics a local butcher shop received a cease-and-desist order from the London Organizing Committee for the Olympic Games (LOCOG) for trademark infringement. LOCOG even had their lawyers accompany the Olympic torch relay in case violations were discovered on the route. More than 80% of those surveyed thought that LOCOG had effectively controlled ambush marketing ("The Sponsorship Effect," 2011).

There are also issues with ambush tactics by athletes themselves. The explosion of social media is causing significant problems for Olympic officials. Rules 40 and 41 in the athlete's code of conduct prohibit athletes from engaging in sponsorship activities (with non-Olympic sponsors) nine days before the Games and three days after. This can clearly be monitored in the traditional media. However, Tweets and Facebook posts are less detectable. This is an issue that will gain considerably more attention and, regrettably, regulation.

There is some concern that the IOC is not practicing what it preaches. In 1994, the IOC developed its own program for IOC sponsors, as opposed to Worldwide Olympic sponsors. The IOC sold an automobile sponsorship to Mercedes-Benz and a clothing deal to Mizuno, among others (Olympic Fact File, 2012). According to one industry leader, "We always thought it a bit underhanded that the International Olympic Committee had its own sponsors" (Ukman, 1998a, p. 2).

The IOC, USOC, NGBs, sponsors, and broadcast networks have worked diligently to curtail ambush marketing of the Olympic Games. In 1996, the Atlanta Organizing Committee, together with the IOC, established a fund to publicize the names of ambush marketers in national newspapers. The advertising copy stated that "Deceptive advertising is not an Olympic sport," and "Every time a company runs an ad like this, our Olympic team loses" (Myerson, 1996, p. D1). These funds were not used and the threat seems to have had the desired results. Currently, the IOC requires the bid cities to enact legislation to control the illegal use of IOC and OOC marks. The IOC reported that, since 1996, the Olympics have been relatively free from serious ambush marketing activities. Skildum-Reid (2012) suggested that a great way to derail ambush markers is to think like an ambush marketer and incorporate those opportunities into your strategies.

Table 4.1. U.S. Television Rights Fees for the Olympic Games

Year	Site	Network	Price
1960	Squaw Valley (Winter)	CBS	$394,000
1960	Rome (Summer)	CBS	$550,000
1964	Innsbruck (Winter)	ABC	$597,000
1964	Tokyo (Summer)	NBC	$1.5 million
1968	Grenoble (Winter)	ABC	$2.5 million
1968	Mexico City (Summer)	ABC	$4.5 million
1972	Sapporo (Winter)	NBC	$6.4 million
1972	Munich (Summer)	ABC	$7.5 million
1976	Innsbruck (Winter)	ABC	$10 million
1976	Montreal (Summer)	ABC	$25 million
1980	Lake Placid (Winter)	ABC	$15.5 million
1980	Moscow (Summer)	NBC	$87 million
1984	Sarajevo (Winter)	ABC	$91.5 million
1984	Los Angeles (Summer)	ABC	$225 million
1988	Calgary (Winter)	ABC	$309 million
1988	Seoul (Summer)	NBC	$300 million
1992	Albertville (Winter)	CBS	$243 million
1992	Barcelona (Summer)	NBC	$401 million
1994	Lillehammer (Winter)	CBS	$300 million
1996	Atlanta (Summer)	NBC	$456 million
1998	Nagano (Winter)	CBS	$375 million
2000	Sydney (Summer)	NBC	$705 million
2002	Salt Lake City (Winter)	NBC	$545 million
2004	Athens (Summer)	NBC	$793 million
2006	Turin (Winter)	NBC	$613 million
2008	Beijing (Summer)	NBC	$894 million
2010	Vancouver (Winter)	NBC	$820 million
2012	London (Summer)	NBC	$1.18 billion
2014	Sochi, Russia (Winter)	Comcast/NBC	$775 million
2016	Rio de Janeiro (Summer)	Comcast/NBC	$1.23 billion
2018	Pyeongchang, South Korea	Comcast/NBC	$963 million
2020	TBD (Madrid, Tokyo, Istanbul)	Comcast/NBC	$1.42 billion

5

Individual Athlete Sponsorships

INTRODUCTION

In "ancient" times, like the 1960s, few athletes were able to obtain individual sponsorship deals. There were salaries for professional players and prize money for tournament winners, yet endorsements were few and far between. Big name players in golf, like Arnold Palmer, Gary Player, and Jack Nicklaus, or tennis stars, such as Billie Jean King and Stan Smith, accorded attention and secured sponsorship deals. However, in 1972, a young, attractive swimmer (who shall remain nameless) won seven gold medals in the Olympics and proceeded to price himself out of the business. This marked a turbulent time in the individual endorsement arena. However, the 1980s marked a revolution in athlete endorsements. The shoe and equipment companies fought over the top players, and endorsement fees escalated through the mid-90s. However, when a recession hit the shoe industry in the later part of that decade, many companies reduced the number of athletes receiving large endorsement fees. The result was that fewer players actually received contracts. This trend carried across sports as the number of PGA players who garnered equipment deals (averaging $250,000) dropped from 50 players to about 20 in 2012 (Mullen & Smith, 2012).

Sadly, this downward trend also applied to U.S. Olympic athletes. Fifty percent of American Olympic track and field athletes (ranked in the top ten) earn more than $15,000 a year in income from their sport. Many struggle to pay their bills (Jones, 2012). British sprinter James Ellinger actually put himself up for endorsement auction on eBay prior to the 2012 Games. World record holder and multiple gold-medalist sprinter Usain Bolt secured a deal with Puma for $40 million just prior to the 2012 London Olympics.

Brooks and Harris (1998) provided a conceptual framework through which sport marketers could examine athletic endorsements. They set forward four classifications of endorsement protocol. The first category was "(a) the explicit mode ('I endorse this product'), (b) the implicit mode ('I use this product'), (c) the imperative mode ('You should use this product'), and (d) the copresent mode (the athlete merely appears in some setting with the product)" (Brooks & Harris, 1998, p. 36). Stone, Joseph, and

Jones (2003) forwarded several factors that corporations should evaluate before selecting athletes for endorsements. They suggest that the athlete should be high in trustworthiness, be easily recognizable by the target audience, be affordable for the sponsor, present little risk of negative publicity, and be well matched with the product. Substantial research has also shown how the fit between an athlete and the products that he or she endorses is a critical factor. Below are several examples to illustrate these points.

ENDORSEMENTS

The lure of sport personalities has existed for decades. Just as Arnold Palmer and Michael Jordan spoke to their generations, action sport athletes Shaun White and Kelly Clark speak to theirs. With the most gold medals and the most total medals in Winter X Games history, Shaun White earned the first Snowboard SuperPipe five-peat in Winter X Games history in 2012. He finished out 2010 with an Olympic Halfpipe Gold medal in Vancouver. Shaun's sponsors include Burton, Red Bull, Target, Oakley, Ubisoft, and AT&T, making him the leading extreme athlete in earnings with $7.5M in annual income ("Shaun White," 2010).

Kelly Clark is the most decorated female Snowboard SuperPipe athlete; she has won eight total medals in her 12 Winter X Games appearances. With an Olympic Gold in 2002 and Bronze from 2010 already under her belt, Clark had a banner season in 2011 where she won nearly every contest she entered, including Winter X Games 15 and Winter X Games Europe Snowboard SuperPipe. At Winter X Games 15, Clark wrote herself into the history books as she became the first female athlete to land a 1080 in SuperPipe competition (Keppler, 2013).

Blazing the trail for other action sport athletes, skateboarder Tony Hawk was among the first to have contracts and endorsements with shoe companies and sport clothiers, as well as his own video game, Pro Skater (Bennett, Henson, & Zhang, 2002; Goldman, 2000). Hawk secured endorsement contracts estimated at $10 million per year, and his video game has been one of the top-selling sports video games in the history of the industry.

Action sports have earned their way into the industry. According to Mickle (2011), the sport landscape has changed a lot. "Kids today are growing up with skating, surfing, and snowboarding as primary options. Two million more kids ride skateboards than play baseball" (Mickle, 2011, p. 5). He predicts that action sport athletes will soon stand on their own as celebrity endorsers.

Michael Jordan defined sport endorsements when he was with the National Basketball Association's (NBA) Chicago Bulls. He serves as the classic example of the way in which a player can build capital through salaries and sponsorship agreements. With a $28 million contract for his playing ability, Jordan could have probably survived, to say the least. But when his contracts from outside endorsements and sponsorships were included, he might even have been considered wealthy. Jordan signed an endorsement deal with Nike worth $20 million per year and, when combined with his other endorsements, his nonsalary earnings rose to $45 million per year in his last year of play. In 2012 Jordan still ranks as one of the most trusted endorsers.

Tiger Woods signed a contract with Nike immediately following his final amateur match. The five-year, $40 million Nike contract was one of the most lucrative in sport endorsement history. After winning the 1997 Master's, he also signed an agreement with Electronic Arts for a video game bearing his name, which remains a strong seller. Tiger still ranked number one in 2008 with $128 million in total earnings ($22.9 million in winnings and $105 million in endorsements). His major sponsors included Gatorade, Buick, TAG Heuer, Gillette, EA Sports, and Accenture [global management and technology company] (Freedman, 2008). However, with his marital problems and hiatus from golf for most of the year, many of his sponsors dropped him as an endorser. Nike, however remained committed. Similarly, 2012 brought disgrace to seven-time Tour De France champion Lance Armstrong when evidence of drug doping was presented by the World Anti Doping Association. When Armstrong did not appear to defend himself, all of his corporate sponsors ended their relations with him, some demanding refunds on fees paid based on contractual behavior clauses.

In this light, the influence of celebrity endorsers is debatable. One survey showed only 4% of consumers said it was very important that a famous person endorsed a product. Other data indicated that over 50% of the public thought athletes did it just for the money (Veltri, 1996). Furthermore, Veltri's research (1996) indicated that, with the exception of Michael Jordan and Tiger Woods, few people were able to match an athlete endorser and the products that he or she endorsed. In general, basketball players were more often accurately recognized than athletes in other sports, and male endorsers were more likely to be recognized than were female athletes (Veltri, 1996).

In the shadow of NBA legend Michael Jordan, LeBron James signed agreements for over $100 million in endorsements during his 2004 rookie season, most notably from his seven-year, $93 million contract with Nike. James signed a variety of deals, including mega-corporations Coca-Cola and McDonald's. James's 2012 earnings totaled $40.5 million (Freedman, n.d.).

The market rebounded after the 2008–09 economic troubles and all of the leading manufacturers expanded their existing and long-term commitments for player endorsements. New to the scene is Chinese shoe manufacturer Li-Ning who, after successful endorsements at the 2008 Beijing Olympics, signed NBA player Dwayne Wade in 2012. Specifically, with the NBA and NFL, the size of the contract for each athlete increased, but the overall number of players under contract did not increase appreciably ("Endorsement Comings and Goings," 2010).

Endorsement earnings are not restricted to the U.S. market. International tennis super star Roger Federer led the 2012 list with just over $45 million in endorsements from Nike, Rolex, Wilson, and Credit Suisse. Others on the list included soccer star Cristiano Ronaldo, who made $22.5 million, with aging star David Beckham holding strong with $37.1 million in endorsement earnings.

Unfortunately for Formula 1 drivers trying to leverage substantial endorsement fees, research shows that only 6% of the exposure value comes from the driver. Thirty-three percent comes from the car and 24% comes from the driver's suit (owned and controlled by the race team). Venerable F1 driver Fernando Alonso had $29 million in salary earnings but only $3 million in endorsements ("Highest-paid Athletes," 2012).

Another issue is that few women made the list of top endorsers. Maria Sharapova was ranked 26th on the international list with earnings of $22 million (TAG Heuer, Prince, Nike) ("Highest-paid Athletes," 2012). Sponsor commitment to women tennis players extends from Nike's Sharapova's 8-year, $70 million (2010–2018) extension to adidas's lifetime contract with Ana Ivanovic (Endorsement Comings and Goings," 2010). Other leading women in endorsement earnings are Danica Patrick (auto racing), skier Lindsey Vonn, and tennis player Serena Williams.

In this age of technology, the profits for endorsements and licensing of players and players' names have evolved from traditional trading cards to video game licensing rights. Basic licensing agreements in professional sport are typically managed by players associations. MLB and the NFL have separate programs run through their respective unions, the Major League Baseball Players Association (MLBPA) and the National Football League Players Association (NFLPA). The National Basketball Players Association (NBAPA) granted all rights to the NBA for $25 million per year plus $8 million for use of the NBAPA logo. The NFLPA earned $19.5 million just from trading cards to produce a total income of $119 million. In the NFL, each player received $53,000 a year in addition to a percentage based on the sale of player-identified items, such as jerseys, posters, and bobbleheads. NFL players receive 10% on player-identified items, but the MLBPA must also pay the League a 15% royalty for use of team names and logos on its deals, as is the case with trading cards, video games, commercials, etc., if team uniforms and logos are used (Kaplan, 2008; "Summary," n.d.).

The MLBPA brought in $16.8 million with another $6.2 million from the league for logo use. Each MLB player received $33,675.03 in 2006 from licensing revenues. EA sports paid the NFL Players Association $35.1 million in licensing rights for games, such as Madden NFL, with $7,500 going to each player based on video game licensing (Kaplan, 2008). Several retired NFL and NBA players have filed litigation over rights fees from "classic" games where their likeness and player number are represented.

CONTROVERSIES

Controversies surfaced during the 1992 Olympic Games when the USA men's basketball team won the gold medal. Several members of the Dream Team had endorsement contracts with Nike, yet Reebok had supplied the U.S. Olympic Committee with its presentation uniforms. Just prior to the medal ceremony, some team members refused to display the Reebok logo during the medal presentations. A compromise was reached wherein players who objected could open the collars of their uniform to cover the logo or drape a U.S. flag over the offending logo. For 1998, the USOC established new, more restrictive, guidelines for logos on team apparel and revised their athlete-participation agreement. The code of conduct introduced for the Athens 2004 Games prohibited athletes from "concealing or covering up a USOC sponsor, supplier, or licensee brand of other identification" (Lombardo, 2004, p. 5). Further complications arose at the 2008 Beijing Olympic Trials when multi-gold medalist U.S. swimmer Michael Phelps was barred from wearing a sponsor's logo on his swim cap. Previously in the 2004 Trials, Phelps and other swimmers had been allowed to have sponsor logos on their caps (Mickle, 2008b).

The twist comes over the controlling body associated with the Olympic Trials. Although USA Swimming conducts the Trials, it does so under the auspices of the USOC. U.S. Swimming claimed that, although their rules had precluded cap logos other than the manufacturer, they had not previously enforced the rule. The USOC, in a position of control, demanded strict adherence to the USOC restrictions (Mickle, 2008b). USA Swimming has responded by proposing new regulations that would allow athletes to wear sponsors logos at USA Swimming events. This would provide an opportunity for swimmers to secure more value for their sponsors (and theoretically make more money). USA Swimming rules would not, however, extend to FINA World Championships or the Olympic Games.

At the international level, the IOC restrictions in place beginning with Beijing 2008 indicate that "no identification other than the manufacturer's logo may appear on any clothing, equipment, or accessories. Pursuant to Rule 53 By-law 1.4 of the Olympic Charter, one identification of the manufacturer per clothing item will be permitted with a maximum size of 20 cm^2" (IOC, 2006).

Another Beijing-related issue arose when the coach of the U.S. Olympic Swim team, Mark Schubert, commented that if you weren't wearing the new Speedo LZR swimsuit, "you'd probably be at home watching the Olympics on NBC." This prompted a law suit from TYR who manufactured a competing swimsuit, citing undue pressure on athletes to wear only suits made by Speedo, the U.S. Swim Team sponsor. U.S. Swimming commented that the last time they checked, the United States was a country with freedom of speech, and Coach Schubert was free to express his opinion (Henderson, 2008, p. 16C). By the way, 90% of all Gold medalists in Beijing wore the LZR suit. It was subsequently banned for London 2012 for providing an undue advantage. For 2013, USA Swimming restructured their sponsorship programs with a nonexclusive apparel category. Speedo was the first to sign on.

The situation for U.S. Olympic athletes is quite complex. The USOC requires athletes to sign a participation agreement that details their responsibility to USOC sponsors. For example, a U.S. athlete is required to wear the official Ralph Lauren clothing for the opening and closing ceremonies. They are required to wear the official Nike gear if they medal and stand on the podium. Agreements with their NGB govern what they wear on the "field of play." This too has its complexities. An NGB such as USA Swimming designates a swimsuit as a performance item. This allows swimmers to wear the suit of their choice (so long as the design and color scheme are approved). However, USA Track & Field and USA Basketball designate shoes as performance gear allowing athlete selection, but restrict the running uniform to NGB control. Just imagine how many duffle bags of gear that an athlete must take to the Games.

There are issues regarding the potential endorsement of women as sex objects. It has been reported that "some elite beach female volleyballers have had their breasts enlarged, and others overtrain their stomach muscles in an effort to obtain the hard, rippled abdomen now touted by the fitness industry as the sexy in-look for women. The intent for both of these body-sculpturing strategies is to use sex appeal to attract an audience to the contests and to attract commercial sponsorship and endorsement contracts" (Brooks, 2001, p. 1). In the early 2000s, tennis player Anna Kournikova was at the center of the controversy. While near the top of women's tennis, she was able to secure endorsements from a variety of companies, but in the process, she began focusing more on her modeling career than tennis and dropped out of the world rankings. Her endorsements, however, continued to rise and seemed to be based predominately on her attractiveness. Her reported earnings exceeded $15 million per year. One of her endorsements was for British company Berlei's Shock Absorber Multiway Sports Bra, a number one seller in Britain, and featured the ad line, "Only the ball should bounce" (McCarthy, 2003). This clearly crossed the line from athleticism to sexism. Fink, Kensicki, Fitzgerald, and Brett (2004) referred to this type of endorsement as "hypersexualized." In their research, they investigated whether a woman's attractiveness or expertise would more effectively influence consumers. Their findings showed that expertise was more effective in establishing a fit between the athlete and the product, and therefore, would better influence consumers. In related research, Brooks (2001) noted, "Marketers using a sexual appeal approach find it very difficult to determine how consumers will interpret this type of message" (p. 3). Brooks contends that "promoting sport by using the female players as a sexual impulse stimulus may not be a profitable, long-term course for either the sport or for the sponsors" (p. 8). As an aside, the use of athletes as sex objects has not been restricted to women. In 2008, soccer start David Beckham was signed by fashion designer Giorgio Armani to endorse its new line of underwear through quite provocative commercials.

Unfortunately, women make considerably less than their male counterparts in sport endorsements. The endorsement leader in women's sport was tennis's Maria Sharapova who reportedly earned $22 million per year ("Highest-paid Athletes," 2012). This included a 10-year, $25 million deal with Prince racquets. The highest women's individual endorsement contract to-date was secured by tennis player Venus Williams who signed a $40 million deal with Reebok. Her sister Serena signed an agreement with Nike in 2003 for a total of $60 million over 8 years (Glase, 2003). Both sisters average about $15 million per year in off-court earnings.

Almost all sports organizations have so-called *billboard* rules regulating the size of sponsor logos that appear on uniforms. The NCAA, NFL, NBA, MLB and NHL all have such legislation. The IOC does as well, but a lesson was learned by the IOC at the 1988 Seoul Olympics: It limited the size of logos on swimming touch pads, starting blocks, and timing devices but not the number of logos. Consequently, timing sponsor Seiko literally covered its equipment with tiny logos.

The NFL stepped up its enforcement of league logo policies: "The League has gone so far as to threaten NFL club equipment managers with fines if players on their teams wear equipment that does not comply with NFL rules. At each game, an NFL inspector will be present to make sure that policies are being followed" (Kaplan, 2007, p. 5). Exceptions, however, have been made. MLB, as noted above, has a rule prohibiting commercial logos on uniforms but has suspended that rule when teams played in Japan. In 2004, the Yankees and the Devil Rays wore Ricoh patches on their sleeves, and in 2008, the world champion Boston Red Sox sported on their sleeves the patch of EMC, a data storage company. In 2012 the NFL allowed teams to sell sponsorship rights on practice uniforms. For example, the Broncos' senior vice president of business development said, "The Broncos are thrilled to align with Buick and GMC, adding these historic brands to our family of corporate partners" ("Broncos Announce," 2012, para. 4). At press time of this book, the NBA was considering allowing teams to sell logo rights on game uniforms.

The dispute over logos has not been confined to team sports. During one U.S. Open tennis tournament, Venus Williams was fined $100 by the Women's Tennis Association (WTA) for refusing to wear the WTA Tour sponsor's patch on her clothing. Williams cited her Reebok contract language which "prohibited any other logo" on her dress (Kaplan, 1998b, p. 9). Interestingly, the WTA rules allowed an exemption for Nike. Williams threatened to sue but ultimately acquiesced. Reebok stayed above the fray, saying that Williams could do whatever she wanted to do (Kaplan, 1998b). In 2003, the ATP relaxed its restrictions on logos. The previous rule was that a player could not wear a non-apparel logo on the front of a shirt, specifically in the case of Visa. If a player had a Nike logo on the front, the player had to put the ATP logo on the back. The modification to the rule allowed non-apparel logos and apparel logos and did not require the ATP logo. However, the four Grand Slam events to date still prohibit non-apparel logos on player shirts. McKelvey noted that these instances "illustrate a growing tension between the desire and the need of sport organizations to regulate and control their business and players, versus the individual freedoms of players, particularly with respect to their pursuit of commercial endorsements" (McKelvey, 2003, p. 3).

The issue of control is so contentious that officials initiated litigation against the NCAA. In 1998, adidas filed suit against the NCAA because it restricted advertising logos by manufacturers, yet allowed its own logos, as well as sport conferences and football bowl sponsors' logos. In thoroughbred racing, several jockeys went to court and won the right to sell advertising on their silks. "I know that there are people who fear that jockeys will now look like logo-covered NASCAR drivers, ruining the majesty and tradition of the Run for the Roses. But if tradition-rich events like the Masters can survive Tiger Woods and the Nike hype machine, the Sport of Kings can withstand a few dollars trickling down to the peasants" (Isidore, 2004). Jockeys, unless they finish in the top three, can go home with as little as $56 for a race.

AGENTS AND AGENCIES

Marketing agents are typically the individuals responsible for helping athletes obtain sponsorships and product endorsements. However, many athletes have other related business and marketing needs. These could include personal appearances and speaking engagements, appearances on screen and in television, print advertising, and investment management. Few individual agents could competently furnish all of the services cited above. Therefore, several companies have been established to offer athletes a package of services from experts in each area. These firms not only represent athletes but provide marketing and sponsorship services, as well as ownership of many major events. Globally, there are other firms engaged in the business as well. Overall, since 2005, there has been a merger of sport representation and celebrity representation in agencies like the Creative Artists Agency (CAA). Since 2007, the CAA has been hiring some of the top athletes' agents and is aggressively pursuing more sport clients. Within a few short years, CAA has become one of the top-ranked agencies in terms of players' salaries. For example, they not only represent Tom Cruise, Will Smith, Jennifer Aniston, and Steven Spielberg, but also Cristiano Ronaldo, Sydney Crosby, Dwayne Wade, Shaun White, Payton and Eli Manning, Derek Jeter, and the ultimate cross-over duo, David and Victoria Beckham. The industry is not, however, free from problems. Another entertainment giant, Wasserman Media Groups, also moved rapidly into athlete representation. IMG has its roots in tennis and golf, since Arnold Palmer in the 1960s, and represents players such as Tiger Woods and Natalie Gulbis in golf, as well as Maria Sharipova and Roger Federer in tennis. Octagon scored big in 2008 representing Olympic swimmer Michael Phelps and his eight gold medal performances. To enable the reader to get a more thorough understanding of agent representation, a sample agent-athlete contract for management has been included at the end of this chapter.

Agent fees can run as high as 5–15% on marketing and endorsement projects. However, U.S. professional leagues' players associations generally restrict agent fees on playing contracts to 3%. The key questions to be asked are, from what monies are the percentage of fees calculated and is the money paid on salary actually paid to the player or to the total value of the negotiated contract?

In fairness to sports agents, most of them do safeguard the best interests of their players. In fact, they often know more about the player's worth than the player does him- or herself. In addition, they have a working knowledge of the types of performance provisions that can go into a player's contract. In the final analysis, agents will be better at negotiating contracts than athletes.

TRENDS

Although there is some sentiment regarding famous players, both team and individual, as effective product endorsers and corporate spokespersons, there are some indicators that the times may be changing. Many of the leading sport shoe manufacturers downsized their endorsement contracts in the late 1990s. For example, Reebok had 130 NBA players under endorsement contracts but reduced the number to 30. While reports suggest the reduction was based on changes in company revenues, some suggested that "brat-like" attitudes and consumer indifference were more likely the cause. Similarly, Nike cut endorsement spending considerably due to a downturn in market conditions and sales, yet terms and payments rebounded in the mid 2000s. The trend also reached into other sport industries. Following the trend that saw sneaker companies slash endorsement contracts, major U.S. golf club manufacturers suffering from sagging sales were cutting back on the number of golfers they pay to carry their clubs.

Companies began to question the credibility and integrity of athlete endorsers. This questioning was accentuated by personal indiscretions (Tiger Woods) and criminal acts (Mike Tyson and NBA player Latrell Sprewell). Tyson was imprisoned for assault, and Sprewell attempted to strangle his coach at a team practice. A few years later Sprewell was said to have told his team owners, "Just tell me how much you are going to fine me for not showing up at your required personal appearances and I'll write you a check." Under the NBA collective bargaining agreement and standard player contract, NBA players must make six personal appearances as requested by the team—similar situations still arise today.

It's unclear where to place the Lance Armstrong situation. The cyclist had all of his Tour de France championships stripped and the debate continues around the fate of his Olympic medals. Although Armstrong never failed a sanctioned drug test, the World Anti-Doping Agency presented significant evidence of his drug use. Armstrong failed to appear at the WADA hearings.

Although not criminal in nature, other athletes' actions also embarrass event organizers and sponsors. 2008 FIS World Cup Alpine Ski champion Bode Miller has presented a variety of challenges for his sponsors. After failing to medal in the 2006 Olympics, several sponsors dropped Miller as a spokesperson, not necessarily based on his performance but on comments made to the media about skiing drunk. For the 2007–2008 season, Miller formed his own support group independent from the U.S. Ski Team, known as Team Bode. However, FIS rules required him to wear the official uniform of the U.S. Ski Team in competitions. Some sponsors were excited to be associated with Miller without having to pay the fee, while others were frightened that they would be caught in difficult situations even though they were not officially affiliated with Miller.

In response to these situations, many endorsement contracts now include special clauses to cover instances where a player or coach is involved in some scandal that reflects negatively on the sponsor. Some contracts reserve the right to terminate an agreement at any time if the commercial value of the endorsee is substantially impaired by the commission of any act that tends to denigrate, insult, or offend the community standards of public morale and decency (Hein, 2003).

In reaction to this, some corporations are turning increasingly to outstanding women athletes for their endorsement options. Women athletes, for the most part, are more accessible than their male counterparts. They are also more open to signing autographs and spending time with young fans. They are also less likely to behave in immoral and unethical ways that might embarrass the company. Stone et al. (2003) noted, "Our study suggests that endorsement opportunities for female athletes are growing and that elite female athletes may now be able to effectively compete with male athletes for some of the lucrative endorsement deals that have traditionally gone to men" (p. 101). The trend is reasonably clear, companies are looking for "squeaky clean" images, and today's women athletes seem to fit the ticket (Gatlin, 2003).

Another reaction to the issues surrounding Tiger Woods and Lance Armstrong has been to seek team and event sponsorships, rather than individual athletes, signaling a future trend. Teams and events were determined by sponsors to have more longevity than players and, thus, are more able to provide extended market influence. Companies are also putting money into the sport itself and events linked with it instead of the individual athletes.

However, just to prove that events are not completely risk free, the 2002 Olympic Games came under U.S. Justice Department investigation for offering bribes to IOC members and their families in an effort to obtain the rights to host the Games. Several sponsors, including Qwest Communications, commented that they were "disappointed in the recent events, the negative press in general surrounding the Olympic movement, and the 'lessening of value' of our substantial commitment" (Finley, 1998, p. 15A).

Irrespective of the problems associated with athlete endorsements, these individual sponsorship arrangements can be effective in marketing products and services in the sport industry. A worksheet for marketing an individual athlete has been included at the end of the chapter. Brooks and Harris (1998) suggested that the most effective endorsements are those that contain a high level of consistency between the image of the endorser and the product or service image. In fact, Boyd and Shank's research (2004) on the effectiveness of endorsements indicated that athletes were most effective when specifically endorsing sports products. This concept supports the contention of McDonald (1998) presented in Chapter 3 and research on the effectiveness of endorsements (Boyd & Shank, 2004) that carefully matched sponsorship and corporate personality as a critical relationship.

In conclusion, here are some of the emerging trends in athlete endorsement (Boland, 2010; Sanders, 2010):

1. Some athletes are accepting sponsor equity (stock shares) in lieu of money. It typically gives them tax advantages as it is taxed as capital gains rather than earned income.

2. Social media activity will be required. No longer will athletes be able to do one commercial shoot and distance themselves from the company.

3. Shorter-term contracts will be the norm. Given the rapidly changing consumer market and the variability of performance, sponsors do not want to get stuck with an unpopular or outdated product.

4. True and authentic engagement with the product will be required. Athletes will have to prove (to the company and the public) that they love the brand and use the products.

5. Stronger morals clauses will certainly dominate the industry. The examples of Tiger Woods, Lance Armstrong, and others have pushed this component into almost every contract.

Best Practice | Sample Personal Financial Management Contract

This agreement is made this _____ day of _____ , 20 ___ , by and between _____ , hereinafter "Player," and _____ , hereinafter "Manager." In consideration of the promises made by each to the other, Player and Manager agree as follows:

1. FINANCIAL MANAGEMENT SERVICES - Manager hereby warrants and represents to Player that he holds college degrees in Business Administration and Law from accredited universities, with sufficient hours of study in Accounting and Marketing to qualify as majors in both fields, and that he has limited experience and training in investments. Player hereby retains Manager to advise, counsel, and assist Player in the management of income generated through Player's occupation as a professional athlete. Manager, serving in a fiduciary capacity, shall act in such a manner as to protect the best interest of Player and ensure effective representation of Player in matters directly and indirectly related to Player's financial situation. Manager shall not have authority to bind or commit Player to enter into any contract or agreement without actual execution thereof by the Player.

Manager shall provide financial management services to the Player as follows: (i) tax planning and preparation of federal and state income tax returns; (ii) assisting Player in determining a satisfactory budget of Player's income on a monthly and yearly basis; (iii) assisting Player in establishing investment goals; (iv) assisting Player in evaluating investment opportunities proposed to Player; (v) assisting Player in securing duly qualified professionals for legal, accounting, estate planning, investment, and insurance services as Player may desire or need.

In the event Manager shall be able to provide professional services set out in (v) above, he must provide said services at the normal rate charged to his clients in said area of professional expertise.

2. FINANCIAL MANAGER'S COMPENSATION - For services provided to the Player pursuant to the terms of Paragraph 1 of this Agreement, above, Player shall pay to Manager an amount that, when added to fees paid to Manager pursuant to the Agreement to represent Player in contract negotiations that was executed on _____ , 20 ___ , shall equal three per cent (3%) of Player's gross income from base salary, signing bonus, reporting bonus, and squad bonus as set forth in his Player's contract for the year in which services are performed, payable as received by the Player from his club.

3. INVESTMENT SERVICES - Manager agrees to keep Player informed of any investment opportunities which the Manager feels may be beneficial to the Player. In the event that the Manager shall secure an investment opportunity for the Player

which the Player desires to acquire, he shall keep accurate statements as to the condition of said investment, and shall report said conditions to the Player no less frequently than every three months, or, if information is not available at such intervals, immediately upon receipt of a status report from the record-keeping source of said investment.

Player may, at his discretion, empower Manager to exercise all rights of ownership with regards to the investments made by Manager on behalf of Player, by executing written documents which specifically set out the powers given to Manager by Player for such matters as collection of income, purchase of additional interests in each said investment, or sale or transfer of said investment.

4. COMPENSATION - Player shall pay to Manager a sum equal to five percent (5%) of the appreciation in value, income received, whether ordinary or capital gain, for each investment made by Manager on behalf of Player.

For purposes of this Paragraph, investments made for Player by a qualified and licensed investment broker secured by Manager for Player shall not be considered to be made by the Manager, and Player shall not be liable for compensation to Manager for income or appreciation in value of said investments.

5. PERSONAL APPEARANCE SERVICES - Manager shall use his best efforts to assist Player in enhancing Player's public image and in assisting Player in securing personal appearances, such as, but not limited to, speaking engagements, commercial endorsements, autograph sessions, promotions, licensing arrangements, and appearances in any mass media outlet. Player shall use such efforts as are reasonably necessary to appear at said opportunities, and to improve speaking and related talents so as to provide a good public image for himself and the organization for which he is appearing.

6. COMPENSATION - For all types of public appearance opportunities secured for Player by the Manager, the Player shall pay to the Manager a sum equal to fifteen percent (15%) of the gross income received by Player for each said appearance. For purposes of public appearance opportunities only, Manager shall be responsible for expenses incurred by him in attempting to secure said opportunities for Player, unless Player agrees in writing to reimburse Manager for expenses incurred on Player's behalf in these matters.

7. EXPENSES - Except as provided in Paragraph 6 above, Player shall reimburse Manager for all expenses that are reasonable and necessary in providing the services on Player's behalf as set out in this Agreement upon receipt of an itemized statement of said expenses from Manager to the Player.

8. ENTIRE AGREEMENT - This Agreement sets forth the entire agreement between the parties hereto and replaces or supersedes all prior agreements between the parties related to the same subject matter. This Agreement cannot be changed orally.

9. TERM - This agreement shall remain in full force and effect for a period of one year from the date above or until the final contract negotiated by Manager for Player with a professional athletic team has expired, whichever shall last occur. However, Player and Manager shall have the right to terminate this Agreement with written notice delivered personally, or by regular United States mail, to the party at his last-known address, and upon the payment of all fees and expenses due hereunder by the terminating party to the other party.

10. GOVERNING LAW - This Agreement shall be construed, interpreted, and enforced according to the laws of the State of _____ .

EXAMINE THIS CONTRACT CAREFULLY
BEFORE SIGNING IT

IN WITNESS WHEREOF, the parties hereto have hereunto signed their names as hereinafter set forth.

_____   _____
AGENT   PLAYER

Individual Athlete Sponsorship Worksheets

The worksheets provide a guide for you in developing various sections of a sponsorship plan. The following sheets cover areas that must be addressed when attempting to secure endorsements for individual athletes. Complete this worksheet as you would prepare a sponsorship plan.

Specify the image, personal likes and dislikes, and speaking abilities of your athlete.

_____
_____
_____
_____
_____
_____
_____
_____

Prepare a list of the products currently used by your athlete.

_____
_____
_____
_____
_____

_____

_____

_____

Identify possible value-in-kind (VIK) opportunities.

_____

_____

_____

_____

_____

_____

_____

_____

Report the specific sport-imposed time constraints that would affect endorsement appearances.

_____

_____

_____

_____

_____

_____

_____

Calculate the relative value of your athlete compared to other athletes.

_____

_____

_____

_____

_____

_____

_____

_____

Brainstorm tentative corporations that could be targeted for consideration.

_____

_____

_____
_____
_____
_____
_____
_____

Research the most likely corporations for approach.

_____
_____
_____
_____
_____
_____
_____

Assemble an "Athlete Package," including a cover letter, athlete
biography, photographs, previous endorsements, and family
background.

_____
_____
_____
_____
_____
_____

Establish a calendar for presenting or mailing packages to potential
corporations and set your allowable response timeline.

_____
_____
_____
_____
_____
_____

Create a checklist to track the results of your efforts.

_____

_____

_____

_____

_____

_____

_____

_____

_____

6

Financial Implications

INTRODUCTION

The finances involved in sports sponsorships are staggering. As mentioned in the first chapter of this workbook, worldwide spending on sponsorship was estimated to be $51 billion in 2012. It's also important to remember that not all sponsorship arrangements involve the exchange of cash. Successful sponsorships often involve trading goods and services that a corporation controls and that the sport organization may need. This has generally been termed *value-in-kind* (VIK), and on average, 40% of all sponsorship agreements encompass at least some provision involving the supply of products and services (IEG, n.d.). Several examples have been presented throughout this workbook. For example, colleges and universities trade sponsorship and signage for uniforms and shoes, and the Olympics accepts computers and data processing in return for sponsorship. Many road races accept energy drinks in return for on-course signage. It is important, however, to heed the words of Mike Mushett, an executive with the 1996 Paralympic Games: "You can't meet payroll with M&M's and Coke" (Mushett, 1995).

What sponsors are looking for is a positive return on their investments. Dannon calculated a positive return on their sponsorship of the Dannon Duathlon Championship Series. Partnering with local grocery stores in each of the eight yearly events, Dannon was able to generate $750,000 from their $250,000 investment ("Dannon Sponsorship," 2003). Ukman (2004b) also provided a breakout of calculating return on investment (ROI) for a boat show that is included at the end of this chapter as a Best Practice.

While many sponsors are demanding a clearer ROI, many experts in the industry are more focused on return on objective (ROO). At a 2008 summit on Sponsorship Measurement, Elizabeth Lindsey, senior VP at the Wasserman Media Group, said that sport sponsorship will never have one standard measure for ROI/ROO but that shouldn't stop disciplined evaluation (Lindsay, 2008). Skildum-Reid (2008a) suggests that "there are some things that can be measured in dollars but most can't. The newest thinking on sponsorship measurement is to shift to the ROO model" (p. 5). This model suggests that corporations establish a budget for the accomplishment involved in specified sponsorship objectives. This would fit nicely with hospitality objectives that are difficult to measure on a dollar-to-dollar basis.

Details of the sponsorship agreement between adidas and the Tampa Bay Buccaneers may provide insight to the seldom-seen financial side of sponsorships (Friedman, 1999, p. 36). The Tampa Bay Buccaneers put together sponsorship packages for their adidas-sponsored stadium. Through a five-year, $1.7 million agreement, adidas agreed to provide $4.4 million in products and $675,000 for community outreach programs. The package included, among other items,

- two 22-by-28-foot trivision panels on each scoreboard,
- one corporate identification (five feet high) above the lower suite level,
- inclusion of the corporate logo in one 16-by-40-foot themed mural in the main stadium concourse,
- signs at six novelty stands,
- one sponsor identification on the score board per quarter of play,
- two full-page advertisements in NFL Insider Magazine,
- periodic mentions in the Buccaneers' newsletter,
- ability to place promotional flyers in stadium cup holders for each game,
- presence on team's Internet homepage,
- one 16-person luxury suite,
- 70 season tickets for all home games (i.e., 10 in club section and 60 in preferred general admission seating sections),
- 16 tickets for the Super Bowl,
- four parking passes,
- one catered tailgate party for 100 guests,
- VIP day for 20 guests at one practice session during the season, and
- one away-game trip per season for four guests (Freidman, 1999).

In this package, no elements were priced individually but rather bundled together with a total price for all components.

PRICING SPONSORSHIPS

The first thing the sport marketer needs to know about pricing a sponsorship is that nobody cares how much money your sport organization needs. Sponsorship consultant Kim Skildum-Reid (2008b, p. 9) said, "The money you need to run an event has nothing to do with its commercial value. Got it? Nothing." Sponsors only care about the value they can get from the partnership. Several different approaches to sponsorship pricing have been utilized extensively in the industry. The following sections address the three most commonly used methods for sponsorship pricing as outlined by Brooks (1994).

Cost-Plus Method

With this technique, you calculate the actual expenses incurred in providing the sponsorship package plus a desired profit for the organization. Costs include all items, including tickets, parking, dinners, souvenirs, and signage. This method has been used effectively by the USOC to price their sponsorship packages. In using this method, be sure to include the labor costs associated with the production of the above elements. In this manner, you will be able to demonstrate to senior management the true profits of the organization.

Competitive Market Strategy

As with any product pricing strategy, you must be competitive with alternative sponsorship options; the problem is trying to discover their price. In the sponsorship business, it is difficult to know the pricing structure of competitors' packages. One of the best ways is to read prominent trade publications. The leading publication on sport sponsorship is the *IEG Sponsorship Report*. This biweekly newsletter covers all of the major activity in the sponsorship industry and includes interviews with industry leaders. For example, the newsletter tracks worldwide spending and reports trends in North America, as well as around the globe. Another noteworthy publication is *SportsBusiness Journal*. While this weekly publication does not focus solely on sport sponsorship, it does present a variety of articles on the topic. The IEG Sponsorship Report systematically lists the prices of all major sponsorship signing on a quarterly basis.

Relative Value Method

This approach to pricing is based on the market value of each sponsorship component. For example, if you are including souvenir program ads in your sponsorship package, you could compare this component to the price and effectiveness of ads in the newspaper. Scoreboard signage could be valued against the cost of billboards, and PA announcements could be equated with radio advertising. You will need to ascertain if the comparison is legitimate and if the same impact can be achieved. This can be accomplished through a review of the cost per thousand (CPM—M representing the Roman numeral for 1,000). Even if your CPM turns out to be higher, you might argue that your audience has a better demographic match to a particular group than it would match the mass media. It has been reported that event-based media elements are somewhat less effective than a direct advertising message. Their suggested value is about 20% of the media cost; however, if the events are provided actual advertising spots during event television broadcasts and legitimate advertising space from a media sponsor, the value would be equal to the full rate offered to other advertisers (Stotlar, 2001; Ukman, 2004c).

Skildum-Reid (2012) suggests that the ratio of media sponsorship should range from 3:1 to 8:1 with more value placed on the media partner than on the cost. Another suggestion indicates that the sponsorship should provide a point of differentiation for the media outlet from their competitors. You should also work within the negotiation process to retain control of the advertising schedule.

In an effort to help event owners justify return on investment to sponsors, one company, Joyce Julius & Associates, has been providing support data for more than 20 years. Their concept was to tabulate the total time that a sponsor's logo appeared on television coverage of major events, and then to provide an exposure value based on the cost of airing a 30-second commercial during the same period. Table 6.1 shows data from the 2012 NASCAR races.

Table 6.1. 2012 NASCAR Sprint Cup Driver Statistics				
Rank/Driver	Exp. Time	Mentions	RG Value	Sightings
1) T. Stewart	2:42:42	24	$13,555,405	2,792
2) B. Keselowski	2:28:34	28	$13,725,430	2,779
3) J. Johnson	2:27:53	18	$10,418,645	2,480
4) M. Kenseth	2:18:54	30	$14,536,390	2,497
5) D. Earnhardt Jr.	2:08:23	20	$17,087,650	1,910
6) J. Gordon	1:45:29	14	$7,926,165	1,688
7) J. McMurray	1:42:14	10	$18,281,870	1,269
8) G. Biffle	1:42:00	18	$12,237,520	1,948
9) C. Edwards	1:41:55	37	$10,980,235	1,507
10) D. Hamlin	1:27:20	33	$10,996,840	1,729

— Statistics reflect live race telecasts and replays of the 2012 NASCAR Sprint Cup Series through Bristol (4 events).

— Each sighting represents one or more seconds of consecutive on-screen time.

Data from the bowl games showed that logo placement on the 20-yard line out-performed mid-field logos 4-to-1. Allstate Insurance, who sponsored both the Sugar Bowl and the BCS Title Championship game, received more than $230 million in value from almost two hours of on-screen exposure (Joyce Julius, 2008).

The NBA Boston Celtics petitioned the NBA to change restrictions on court-side signage such that the 30-foot center court signage could be broken into two 10-foot signs at each end of the floor, and on the 25-foot center scores table sign. Their research indicated that, since most of the play occurs at the end of the courts, television exposure would increase by 250% (Lombaro, 2008).

Some have argued that the same advertising message cannot be delivered in on-screen logo presence as can be presented in a 30-second ad. However, that rationale fails if channel surfers and TiVo users are accounted for since they don't watch the commercials but are exposed to in-event messages. Perhaps a smart strategy is to use a ratio to assess the value of such exposure. IEG suggests that sponsors apply a 1-to-5 ratio in decreasing the value for on-screen logo appearance versus the actual cost of the commercial (Ukman, 2004c).

Sponsors have also been known to use all of these price valuation methods for analyzing proposed sponsorship packages. NationsBank's sport and event marketing vice president said, "When I receive a proposal, I do a payout analysis, putting dollars against each benefit the property is offering" (Goldberg, 1998, p. 29).

Collateral Support

To sufficiently support a sport sponsorship, corporations must be willing to spend additional dollars promoting their involvement. Estimates vary among corporations on the amount of additional spending that will be required to increase visibility of the sponsorship and that will be needed to activate consumers. The general rule is that a sponsor must be willing to spend at least an amount equal to the rights fee of their sponsorship to leverage the effect (Skildum-Reid, 2012). Nextel's $45 million-per-year title sponsorship of NASCAR included a sponsor commitment to spend a like amount on marketing their relationship (Rovell, 2004). Coca-Cola estimates its ratio as 5-1, spending $5.00 on promotions and advertising for every $1.00 it spends on sponsorship fees. AT&T spent six times the cost of their sponsorship to make their sponsorships "known to employees and felt by customers" (Ukman, 1998c, p. 2). Other authorities recommend that, at a minimum, sponsors spend an amount at least equal to the sponsorship fee for promotion and leveraging (Skildum-Reid, 2012; Stotlar, 2001). A sponsorship alone, which is without collateral support, will rarely produce the desired results. The partnership must be leveraged through all of the sponsor's and the organization's assets.

SMALL BUDGET SPONSORSHIPS

In most small companies or divisions, the budget doesn't include a spare $750,000 to get involved in high-priced sport sponsorships. However, several companies have been successful in low budget sponsorships that have produced good results. Even at the Olympic level, sponsors can get in for a modest amount of money. By sponsoring U.S. Speed Skating for the 2002 Winter Olympic Games, uniform sponsors were able to have their logo appear on the cover of *Sports Illustrated* when Casey Fitzrandolf won a gold medal in the 500m. A full-page color ad in *Sports Illustrated* costs over $300,000, but there is no price for the cover. In another example, Bavarian Coachworks, a company specializing in customized Porsches, spent only $40,000 to get prime ad placement on a racecar entered into 17 events. The shop owner credited the ad with increasing his business 60–70%, many times the cost of the sponsorship. Local auto racing can be even cheaper as some drivers will almost give ad space away just so they can look like "real" sponsored racers.

At some point, the sport marketer has to ask for money from the sponsor (more detail on specific strategies will be presented in Chapter 8). It's much easier if the marketer has presented the financial benefits in a clear and precise manner. The sport marketer provides a service, a true benefit that can be measured in dollars and is not asking for a charity handout. One major problem occurs when the money is hypothetically put on the table. If a sponsor offers $30,000 for a $100,000 package, the sport marketer has to walk away. A good package will stand on its own merit. With this business approach and attitude, a positive response is likely. An effective sport marketer has the data to show that sport sponsorship doesn't cost—it pays.

Best Practice — Calculating Return on Sponsorship

The following example was constructed by IEG (Ukman, 2004b, p. 4) as a best practice in calculating return on sponsorship. The scenario details the results for an automotive manufacturer's $50,000 sponsorship of a boat show in which the primary objective was to increase sport utility vehicle (SUV) sales.

Boat show attendance	=	40,000
Attendees who visited booth and pick-up test drive offer	=	14,000
Booth visitors who visited dealer for a test drive (7%)	=	980
Test drivers who purchased within a 12-month period (12%)	=	118
Average profit per vehicle	=	$2,000
Gross profit from sponsorship	=	$236,000
Rights fees	=	$50,000
Production and promotion costs	=	$50,000
Net profit	=	$136,000
Return on investment	=	136%

Financial Worksheets

The worksheets provide a guide for you in developing various sections of a sponsorship plan. The following sheets cover the financial aspects of pricing a sponsorship. Complete this worksheet as you would prepare a sponsorship plan.

Calculate a price for your sponsorship using the cost-plus method.

Compare the market value of similar sponsorships with your cost-plus calculations above and evaluate the need for any adjustments in pricing your sponsorship.

_____

_____

_____

_____

_____

_____

_____

_____

_____

Complete a relative value calculation by examining the media and retail tie-in portions of your sponsorship (if applicable) and evaluate the need for any adjustments in pricing your sponsorship.

_____

_____

_____

_____

_____

_____

_____

_____

_____

Examine the needs that your organization may have for sponsor products or services and prepare a list of possible value-in-kind (VIK) contributions and their appropriate value.

_____

_____

_____

_____

_____

_____

_____

_____

7

Developing Successful Sport Sponsorship Proposals

INTRODUCTION

This chapter will present an overview and a conceptual model for development of sport sponsorship proposals derived from field-based applications. Specific examples and procedures will be examined and presented to you for use as models in building sponsorships for your sport organization.

Sport has proven its revenue potential as a marketing vehicle, and the sponsorship proposal is the essential element for this process. The task of the sport manager lies in presenting a proposal that specifically identifies sponsors' benefits and needs (discussed in Chapter 3); however, it cannot be stressed enough that corporations are looking for flexibility in proposals, not set bundles of components. One corporate executive commented, "Most properties package what they need to sell without thinking what has value for their partners" (Goldberg, 1998, p. 29). The preferable strategy carefully examines each sponsor and uncovers the requisite needs for each potential sponsor.

IEG Sponsorship Report is one of the best sources for accessing information on the inside operations of companies sponsoring sport events (referenced earlier in the workbook). This Chicago-based, biweekly publication from the International Events Group (IEG) provides detailed analyses of sponsorship packages and the attendant framework. They also frequently list requests for sponsorship proposals from a variety of corporations.

Getting information about potential sponsors is essential. If the company is a publicly traded company, it is required to file an annual report with the Securities and Exchange Commission (SEC). Annual reports filed with the SEC can be accessed through their website (www.sec.gov) and through the Public Register's Annual Report Service (www.prars.com). Each of these sources can provide valuable data for use in structuring a sponsorship proposal.

In an effort to deal with an increasing number of proposals, many corporations prefer the online submission of sponsorship proposals and some corporations have developed specific criteria for proposals. A sample online proposal format has been modified from several online sites and provided in Figure 7.1. Other corporations will consider any reasonable format devised by the event or property owner. In addition, excerpts and

Name of the Event

Event Management Contact

Name

Title

Address

Phone

FAX

Email

Event Management Experience

Event Location(s)

Venue

Description of the Event

Image Match and Integration

Number of Events

One-time only . . . . _____

Series of events . . . . _____

Duration of the Event

Proposed date(s) . . . . _____

Audience size . . . . _____

Audience Demographics

Gender profile . . . . _____

Percentage in Age Groups

Percentage in income brackets _____

Ethnicity profile . . . . _____

Lifestyle characteristics
(AOI) . . . . _____

Media Profile (specify coverage under contract, historical data, or projected coverage)

TV . . . . _____

Newspaper . . . . _____

Radio . . . . _____

Promotional Plan (specify coverage type, length, units, frequency, production details, and sponsor's access)

TV . . . . _____

Newspaper . . . . _____

Radio . . . . _____

Website . . . . _____

Direct mail . . . . _____

Database . . . . _____

PR events . . . . _____

Live marketing event(s) . . . . . _____

Level of Sponsorship (title, presenting, supplier, etc.)

Sponsorship Category, Parameters, and Exclusivity

Former Sponsors (list company, category, level, and year)

Existing and Proposed Sponsors (list company(s), category, and level; indicate if under contract or proposed)

Sponsorable Components and Benefits

Signage . . . . _____

Venue messaging . . . . _____

Tag to media advertising . . . . . _____

Hospitality (suites, tickets,
passes, parking, food and
beverages) . . . . _____

Pre-event activities . . . . _____

In-event activities . . . . _____

On-site product trial . . . . _____

On-site display . . . . _____

On-site product sales . . . . _____

Ceremonies . . . . _____

Celebrity/athlete/VIP access
or appearance . . . . _____

Value-in-kind (VIK)
opportunities . . . . _____

Cross-promotion opportunities . _____

Licensing . . . . _____

Post-event activities . . . . _____

Other . . . . _____

Identified Measures for Evaluation Report

Rationale (why and how each benefit is appropriate fit to the sponsor)

Proposed Budget and Value of Benefits

Figure 7.1. Sponsorship Submission Format Model

sample wording from an authentic sponsorship proposal have been included at the end of the chapter in Best Practice.

The level of sophistication has increased as the industry has matured throughout the last ten years. Accordingly, few boilerplate sponsorship proposals have been effective. In other words, in an effort to save time, some sport properties have attempted to create a boilerplate proposal to distribute to multiple sponsors. These boilerplates usually contain the entire inventory that the organization has collected from their sponsorship; however, little attention is given to molding this package into the right framework for the targeted corporation. A simple "cut and paste" approach is taken in order to generate as many proposals as possible. As Lauletta, director of sports and event marketing for Miller Brewing Company, said, "I still receive proposals with Coors and Heineken's names in place of Miller and it always amazes me how lazy someone can be" (Lauletta, 2003, p. 8). Recipients easily expose this generic approach and the proposal is most likely discarded.

In putting together a sponsorship proposal, Ukman (1995a) suggested several attributes that should be addressed in a quality sponsorship proposal. She emphasizes that the proposal should promote benefits, not package features. Company executives are looking for promotional platforms that can effectively produce quantifiable advantages for the company. Therefore, the focus of the proposal should be on the sponsor's, not the property's, needs. Ukman indicated that too often the proposal spends an inordinate amount of space detailing why the organization needs the money or how important it is to stage the event.

"The successful proposal is tailored to the sponsor's business category. Boilerplate proposals do not work" (Ukman, 1995a, p. 2). As discussed in Chapter 3, specific attributes of a proposal may meet the image needs of one company but another company may need product sampling. The sport marketer should work hard to establish a pre-proposal meeting in an effort to determine the specific needs of their prospects. The VP for NBA analytics commented that "to measure what our sponsors care about, we must understand their business objectives and planned activations" (Seiferheld, 2011, p. 15). They must do their homework and have a high level of understanding about the potential sponsor in order to actively participate in a discussion of their needs. Only then can an effective sponsorship proposal be developed. The proposal should also explain how benefits can be leveraged through the sponsor's existing marketing programs to achieve extended impact. Finally, the best proposals communicate the advantages of alliances and strategic partnerships that will ultimately provide greater utility than either party could accomplish separately (Ukman, 1995a).

SPONSORSHIP DESCRIPTION

The first step in developing an outstanding sponsorship proposal is the description of the event or property offered by the organization. This includes the history, years of organizational operation, and structure of the sport enterprise. Major corporations want to know the kind of organization with which they are getting involved. As pointed out at the New York-based Sports Summit, "If we are going to sponsor an event, I want to see the financial history of the people putting things together. How much can they cover? Is this event really going to come off? I know this sounds stupid, but too many people never ask that question. Those are the ones that get burned" (Macnow, 1989, p. 39).

PROPOSAL OBJECTIVES AND MATCH TO SPONSOR NEEDS

As previously mentioned in Chapter 3, a match must be made between corporate objectives and the opportunities available through the sponsorship arrangement. Therefore, the objectives of the proposal must be clearly presented in relation to how the sponsorship will benefit the sponsor. Specific objectives must be delineated regarding target market demographics, psychographics, image opportunities, awareness strategies, market share increases, and business-to-business relationships.

Just as marketing practices have changed from a product orientation to a market orientation, sponsorships have changed, as well. In the early days of sponsorship, properties would put together "Gold, Silver and Bronze" style packages and offer them to potential sponsors. Those days have long ago passed and the need for flexibility and customization is essential. All too often, properties are intent on selling their inventory of sponsorable components, rather than presenting options to a potential sponsor that the property needs. Respondents in Seaver's 2004 corporate survey advised marketers to align sponsorship proposals to meet the business objectives of prospective sponsors. Attention to these factors can result in a longstanding sponsorship association.

SPONSORABLE COMPONENTS

The available components of sponsorship should be presented to the sponsor in detail. Every available activity or planned event should be described, including the corporate opportunities available within each activity or event. These should be linked to standard business practices that have been proven to produce results. In addition, these results should be clearly tied to actionable components of the sponsorship. For example, most corporations have a positioning strategy in place. A proposal should describe how the features of the sponsorship could solidify the organization's corporate position in the mind of the consumer.

A good place to start is to reexamine the needs for sponsors, presented in Chapter 3. When examining what sponsors want, the sport marketer will need to conduct an audit of the benefits that the organization has to offer. There are, of course, the natural elements surrounding the sport organization, such as stadium signage, the title of an event or activity, and the advertising linked to the organization's communication outlets (e.g., game/event program ads, television, newspapers, and websites). However, with a little creativity, features like a newsletter, Facebook page, Twitter feeds and access to a customer database can really pull the sponsor into a sport organization and create a true partnership (it is recommended that if the organization doesn't already have newsletters, a Facebook page or customer database, the sport marketer should help to create one). Sport properties also have a great opportunity to assist with product displays and product sampling. As noted with the U.S. Swimming sponsorship by a sunscreen product, the manufacturer wanted to get its product into the hands of its target market. In another case, auto dealers were able to capitalize on grassy areas of the football stadium for vehicle display during their prime new model introduction period with no added costs for the organization. Other assets, like hospitality, inclusion in PR events, and permission to co-promote with your logo, are great additions to a sport marketer's inventory.

One of the best features about sport is an inventory that cannot be duplicated by many other industries. Of course, sponsors can buy television exposure and ads in newspapers and on websites, but they can't buy access to players and coaches or behind the scenes tours in sport venues. Canon, who had been a longstanding NFL sponsor, has found a high level of success with its "Shoot Like a Pro" program. Amateur photographers enter the contest on Canon's (or the NFL team's) website for a chance to win game tickets and sideline passes for a selected game. Photos are taken with the latest Canon camera and the amateur gets tips from a professional photographer. These are benefits that were created especially for specific sponsors. It was creative and effective and had no added sponsorship costs.

Sports teams also have the benefit of providing access to game-used items, like game-worn jerseys and game balls for sponsors. While there is a cost related to providing these items, it easily can be offset through the price of the sponsorship. These special benefits are an important part of a sport marketer's inventory. They create meaning for the fans and help transfer the emotion from the sport to the sponsor. Also, when a sport marketer combines sponsorable components, they must truly differentiate those compo-

---

Sample Inventory

Sponsorship Types
Title sponsor
Presenting sponsor
Naming rights (for awards, facility – sections, subordinated event, or an entire day)
Official product or supplier

Exclusivity
At given levels
Within certain categories (define them clearly)

License and Endorsement
Use of event or team logo in their advertising
Official product status

On-site
Sampling opportunities
Product demonstrations and displays
On-site sales or merchandising

Signage
Venue locations (size and location specific)
Vehicles
Participant and/or staff uniforms or number tags
Flags or banners

Hospitality
Tickets to the event
VIP parking or shuttle service
Access to specified VIP areas
Access to specified VIP activities ("money cannot buy" experiences)
Customized VIP experiences and events

Technology
Banners and content on your website with links to their sites
Web-based promotional events

Loyalty Marketing
Special parking or access to their customers (e.g., several stadiums have Lexus parking zones)
Early access to tickets (e.g., American Express arranged this with tennis's U.S. Open)
Access to special blocks of seating

Database Marketing
Access to event or organization database
Promotional flyers in event or organization mailings

(adapted from Grey, A. M., & Skildum-Reid, K. (2007). *Sponsorship seeker's toolkit* [2nd ed.]. Sydney, Australia: McGraw Hill.)

nents that fall under higher levels of sponsorship from those in lower categories. Multiple factors and components differentiating a $100,000 from a $50,000 sponsorship should be considered; for example, the $100,000 sponsorship should produce more than just twice as many stadium signs.

It is also essential that the responsibility for developing each aspect should be clarified. If corporate hospitality is a primary feature of the proposal, who will provide the catering must be verified. Typically, the event or property provides the facility and arranges the dialog with approved caterers. Ultimately, it is the sponsor who selects the menu and finalizes the service protocol and details.

PRICING

The presentation of cost estimates has been an area where many sports organizations have encountered difficulties. Pricing can be prepared for either an entire proposal or for specific options within the proposal. For most sponsors, flexibility is the key.

The most important step in pricing is making an accurate valuation. Therefore, the pricing methods presented in Chapter 6 are critical. Each potential sponsor is engaged in other marketing activities, each of which has a price and value. The sport manager must study and prepare data that demonstrate and accurately translate the benefits of sport sponsorship in terms the corporation can understand. As noted in Chapter 6, it is also important to remember that industry experts estimate an incremental commitment on the part of the sponsor in order to integrate the sponsorship with their existing marketing functions. These can range from an additional 100–500% of the sponsorship cost.

Many managers have found one aspect of sport sponsorship difficult to foresee: Often, corporations would rather deal with large projects than be victimized by a multitude of small ones (see Fewer, Bigger, Better in Chapter 1). Many sponsorship executives believe that high dollar deals are more profitable and less work that numerous small ventures. Therefore, it is important to offer the company several options in their sponsorship agreement, ranging from exclusive ownership of all events and opportunities to smaller and less expensive options such as value-in-kind (VIK) provisions or associated advertising.

PREPARATION OF THE PROPOSAL

There has been some debate regarding the actual appearance of the sponsorship proposal. Some practitioners believe that a quality proposal should have the logo of the sport entity and the sponsor's logo prominently displayed on the cover of the proposal. However, others have cautioned that sponsors may react negatively if their corporate logo is used without permission and lead them to question the ethical behavior of the organization. No clear-cut model exists, but a conservative approach would support a professionally prepared proposal without the sponsor's logo. If you are able to arrange a pre-proposal meeting, permission to use their logo may be secured. Another issue arises in the quality of the printing used for the proposal materials. Some authorities have suggested that organizations should prepare the highest quality materials that they can afford. This would include full-color, glossy brochures detailing all of the benefits. On the other hand, some sport marketers believe that the material should be of a more moderate quality to leave the impression that the organization is not frivolous in its spending. The author supports producing the highest quality possible and securing VIK when available to obtain the materials.

The model presented above and the examples shown at the end of the chapter have been derived from existing sponsorship proposals and agreements, and they can provide sport marketers with the skills necessary to succeed in the exciting world of sponsorship.

Best Practice	**Honda Center Partnership Opportunities**
	(Excerpts Depicting Selected Sponsorship Plan Elements)

Event Management

The Honda Center ranks second in the country and third in the world in gross ticket sales behind only London's 02 Arena and New York's Madison Square Garden. Rounding out the Top Five were Sydney, Australia's Acer Arena, and the Thomas & Mack Center in Las Vegas.

Image

Honda Center stands as one of the premier entertainment and sports venues in the country by annually welcoming an average of 1.7 million guests. The Honda Center has welcomed 144 total events, including 33 concerts, since its opening.

Signage/Exposure

The 57 Freeway Marquee adds state-of-the-art visibility for Honda Center to the 64 million cars that are seen annually, and it recognizes every partner on its marquee through highly visible, backlit ad panels. The 25-by-27-foot digital LED screen displays rotating messages about upcoming events, as well.

Katella Marquee: The East Katella marquee provides up-to-date information about all Honda Center events. The marquee has quality branding opportunities available on the four backlit panels. There are two panels on each side of the marquee providing visibility to both east-bound and west-bound travelers 24 hours a day.

Scoreboard Signage: The Honda Vision scoreboard provides quality branding opportunities through the following signage elements:
- Four (4) upper panels
- Four (4) lower panels

In-Bowl Signage
- Four (4) corner panels
- Four (4) center scoreboard panels

LED Signage
- Two (2) 360-degree LED rings offer fully animated, high impact branding opportunities through logo, graphics, and feature presentations

- In addition to exclusive LED visibility during Ducks' games

All-Arena LED partners will receive four (4) minutes of 360-degree LED visibility during the ingress and egress of all nonhockey Honda Center events:

The following are recently created opportunities that give exposure to millions of guests year round:

- Center, East, and West Honda-vision screens
- Naming rights of club level
- Outer walls of club level
- East and West backlit panels
- East and West scrolling ad panel units

Additional signage opportunities:
- LED ring under Honda-vision
- North and South scrolling panel ad units
- Hockey signage
- Dasherboards
    > Corner dasherboards
    > End-zone dasherboards
    > Mid-zone dasherboards
    > Neutral-zone dasherboards
- Team bench and penalty box
- Signage behind Ducks bench and away team penalty box
- Signage behind away team bench and Ducks penalty box
- Player tunnels
- One (1) sign above Ducks player tunnel
- One (1) sign above away team player tunnel
- Zamboni machine tunnel
- Zamboni machine wrap
- Branding representation on Zamboni® machines utilizing a full wrap
- Two (2) total Zamboni® machines on the ice at once
- Visibility to all fans during pre- and post-game and two intermissions

Integrated Communications:
- Placement of sponsor's branded logo on the hondacenter.com website.
- High visibility to all website visitors throughout the year.
- Creation of customized sponsor webpages and content.
- Logo inclusion on more than 175 integrated customizable screens, including 50 HD screens that will specifically target patrons to help increase brand awareness.
- Branding opportunities exist by utilizing 30-second commercial units, as well as static branding messages, bordering the screens of each television in the arena. Screens are located throughout the Plaza level concourse, club level, and all suites.

Ducks Media

Television Exposure for the Season:
- 41 games on FSN and PrimeTicket,
- 14 games on KDOC,
- 23 games on FSN West,
- 4 games on Versus.

Television Elements on Select Broadcasts:
- In-game features,
- 30-second ad spots,
- Opening/closing billboards.

Radio Elements:
- AM 830 will be the flagship station for all 82 Ducks games,
- In-game feature,
- 30- and 60-second in-game spots,
- 30- and 60-second pre- and post-game spots,
- Opening and closing billboards.

Media Shows:

Sponsorship opportunities for both The Element and DucksTV exist in title sponsorship, ad spots, broadcast features, and other elements that can be mutually developed.

The Element, the official magazine show of Honda Center, is broadcast over the air to more than 6 million viewers in Los Angeles and Orange County areas. The show consists of four segments with two- to three-minute commercial breaks.

DucksTV
- DucksTV is the first ever preproduced webcast in the NHL. Last year 54 shows were shown with an average monthly viewing of 14,000.

Honda Center Attendee Demographics

Gender
51% male viewers
49% female viewers

Age
39% adults ages 18 to 24
61% adults ages 35 and older
75% adults ages 18 to 49

HHLD Income
77% of viewers earn $50,000 or more
64% of viewers earn $75,000 or more
46% of viewers earn $100,000 or more

Household
54% of viewers are married
56% of viewers have 1 or more children
70% of viewers own a residence

Education
72% of viewers have a college degree or above
14% of viewers have a post-graduate degree

Race
62% of viewers are White
20% of viewers are Hispanic
6% of viewers are Asian
6% of viewers are Black
6% of viewers identify with another racial group

Hospitality
- Private, catered suite parties are available in the exclusive Party Suite.
- Season tickets, club tickets, and single game tickets can be purchased.
- Players and team management personnel are available for exclusive dinners and VIP functions.
- Passes to the VIP Blue Line Lounge are provided.
- Sponsorship of in-game promotion during Ducks' games is encouraged. Brand presence can include logo recognition on the LED and Honda Vision, PA announcements, and product displays.

Note: Sincere appreciation is extended to Bob Wagner, senior vice president and chief marketing officer for the Anaheim Ducks, for sharing the above sponsorship package information.

Sponsorship Proposals Worksheets

The worksheets guide the development of various sections of a sponsorship proposal. The following sheets cover the creation of a sponsorship proposal. Complete this worksheet as you would prepare a sponsorship plan.

Provide an overall description of the sponsorship.

_____
_____
_____
_____
_____
_____
_____

Describe the organizing committee and/or management attributes of your staff.

_____

_____

_____

_____

_____

_____

_____

_____

_____

Present the similarities of demographic profiles between the sponsor's customers and your event or property.

_____

_____

_____

_____

_____

_____

_____

_____

Detail the match in psychographic characteristics between the sponsor's customers and your event or property.

_____

_____

_____

_____

_____

_____

_____

_____

Project the anticipated media coverage or evaluate the previous media coverage.

_____

_____

_____

_____

_____

_____

_____

_____

List the activities included in the proposal that are designed to
enhance sponsor awareness.

_____

_____

_____

_____

_____

_____

_____

_____

_____

List the opportunities included in the proposal that are designed
for image building.

_____

_____

_____

_____

_____

_____

_____

_____

_____

Specify elements in the proposal designed to drive sales of
sponsor products and services.

_____

_____

_____

_____

_____

_____

_____

_____

Determine the potential for retailer and/or wholesaler tie-ins.

_____

_____

Describe the sponsorship events for developing hospitality relationships.

Examine aspects of the sponsorship that could be used for employee motivation.

Enumerate each of the sponsorable components within the proposal.

Calculate the price of the entire sponsorship for each component in the proposal.

_____
_____
_____
_____
_____
_____
_____
_____
_____

Identify each of the other current sponsors.

_____
_____
_____
_____
_____
_____
_____
_____
_____

Delineate possible risks and your organization's plan to minimize those risks.

_____
_____
_____
_____
_____
_____
_____

8

Securing Sponsorship Agreements

INTRODUCTION

One of the most difficult decisions you will face after the development of your sponsorship plan will be based on determining a contact for a particular company. In the industry, this is referred to as the Access or Point of Entry. There has been considerable confusion over the most successful approach to sponsorship acquisition. Recent research ("IEG Survey: Cold Call Rules," 2007, p. 1) indicates that sponsorships are most often secured through the following entry channels:

55% . . . The property approaches the sponsor, known as a cold call.
19% . . . The property hires an agency who approaches the sponsor.
13% . . . The sponsor contacts the property directly.
8% . . . The property board member contacts the sponsor.
5% . . . Other entry channels are used.

It is surprising to see the high percentage of the sponsorships that were secured through a cold call. Cold calls result either from an actual telephone call to the sponsor's organization or from providing an unsolicited proposal through the mail. One of the biggest shock waves through the industry occurred when the $750 million NASCAR title sponsorship with Sprint started through a cold call. According to Migala (2003), for anyone selling sports sponsorships, cold calling is easily one of the most dreaded aspects of their job. Migala's advice is that, before you call, you should relax and take 30 seconds to think about what you want to get across. The consensus of the sponsorship buyers he interviewed was that most sellers do not take even a few minutes to think and prepare for a few of the situations that might be waiting on the other end of the line. It is important to have a real sense of why this property is a good fit beyond the obvious reasons. One executive said, "If you are going to make the call, then be prepared. I often get people that say they thought they were going to get voicemail and weren't prepared to have a live conversation. That's no way to start a relationship." Universally, the best beginning to any live conversation is to simply ask the person if it is a good time to talk (Migala, 2003, p. 4).

Voicemail is a way of life. Therefore, voice messages are an important part of the way we communicate. Below is an example of a message that one industry executive thought was effective. "Good morning, [name]. I am sorry to bother you. I know it is a crazy time for you, as always, but I want to introduce myself to you over the phone when you have a few minutes. I work for a minor league baseball team in Florida, and even though my research of your marketing activities may or may not lead to a sponsorship immediately, I know that we may meet each other in the future and I would like to start a dialogue when you have time" (Migala, 2003, p. 5). Sponsors would consider this message to be ineffective.

Migala (2007b, p. 4) presented the top reasons cited by sponsors for not returning a call:

1. The message was all about the property not the brand.
2. The caller was not confident.
3. The caller mentions a competing brand—that alone is enough to delete the message.
4. The caller does not detail the next steps (for example, "I'll call you back on . . .," or "I'll send additional information.").
5. The caller does not leave a return phone number.
6. The caller phones from their cell phone, a no-no on the first call.

All corporations handle sponsorship solicitation differently since the volume of calls is tremendous. Some corporations get as many as 3,000 proposals per year (Seaver, 2004). Recently, many corporations have moved to Web-based proposal submission procedures. General Motors has been using an electronic submission process since 1999. Through their in-house marketing agency, GM*R Works, they require applicants to complete forms that detail pertinent information about the sponsorship opportunity. Miller Brewing Company also uses an in-house agency but adds a corporate software filter for their proposals.

Some have a localized decision network where the distributor in the area has the authority to make decisions related to sponsorship. In other cases, all sponsorship decisions must be approved at the corporate headquarters. One executive who was seeking a sponsorship deal and who had extensive experience in working with soft drink and beer sponsors, approached a camera company in the same manner. He knew that the soft drink and beer companies would not consider a sponsorship unless there was a considerable amount of support from local retailers and regional distributors. Unfortunately, after obtaining the backing of field offices for the camera manufacturer, he went to the corporate headquarters only to find that the headquarters didn't like the tail wagging the dog.

A thorough investigation of the business structure is certainly warranted for each potential sponsor. Coca-Cola, for example, selects 95% of its sponsored events at the local level. So, a sport marketer should not send a proposal to Atlanta without enlisting the support of the local bottler. A thorough analysis of point-of-access alternatives is becoming more important as corporations are being deluged with requests and many are not accepting unsolicited sponsorship proposals.

PREPARING A COVER LETTER

Typically, after a sport marketer has identified the appropriate point-of-access, one of the first steps is preparing a cover letter. Allen (1998) suggested that a cover letter sent with a sponsorship proposal can often make the difference between getting a sponsorship package read and getting a nice thanks-but-no-thanks letter. She suggests several trusted rules that should be followed when composing a cover letter (Allen, 1998):

1. Make sure that you send the letter to the proper person at the corporation. Spell their name correctly and list their appropriate title. If you don't know this information, call the company switchboard for assistance.
2. Use compelling terminology as opposed to less effective phrases. Examples of helpful phrases include "measurable response," "reinforce market position," "increase market share," "solidify client relationships," and "integrate marketing opportunities."
3. Make sure that your letter is focused on individually tailored benefits for the recipient. Some of the letters can be from a template, but the body must be customized for each sponsor with benefits matched to fit the sponsor's needs.
4. Do not make overly general statements that cannot be supported by facts. For example, don't say, "All of the media outlets are excited about this event." Rather, you should indicate which specific media have agreed to cover the event.
5. Never shift the responsibility for a followup to the sponsor (e.g., "I look forward to hearing from you"). Instead, thank the reader for their time and indicate that you will call them the following week for further discussions regarding the proposal.

Skildum-Reid (2012) notes that too often sponsors who receive proposals are not direct enough with those seeking their support. They typically comment, "Our funds are currently committed," rather than addressing the weakness of the proposal. She believes that a more direct critique of the proposal will ultimately result in properties developing better proposals. For instance, she suggests that the sponsor could say, "We don't consider uncustomized proposals as it shows that you haven't researched our brand and target market needs. Feel free to review our online sponsorship guidelines and resubmit if you feel there is a fit." She provides another possible comment: "It looks like you are really after a philanthropic donation. If we are going to invest marketing funds, we need to see a substantial opportunity to meet marketing and investment objectives."

SPONSORSHIP PROPOSAL PRESENTATIONS

The following model (Figure 8.1) has been used extensively in many sales situations and seems to work exceptionally well in selling sponsorships. The model begins with establishing your credibility, moves to the identification of challenges, explains how the sponsorship can provide solutions, and concludes with the pricing information.

As mentioned in Chapter 3, corporations may be hesitant to allow their image, trademarks, and brands to be managed by an unproven sport organization. Therefore, building credibility (known as Phase I) is essential in securing the corporation's trust. The ad-

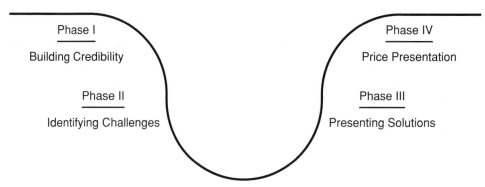

Figure 8.1. Sponsorship Presentation Model

vertising slogan of the first worldwide Olympic sponsorship program was "a company is judged by the company it keeps." A multitude of factors can lead to the establishment of credibility, including business mannerisms, acceptable protocol, previous performance history, and testimonial evidence. Notwithstanding these factors, personal charm and charisma also contribute to building trust.

Phase II of the process involves an open review of challenges that the potential sponsor may face. The biggest mistake that properties make when presenting proposals to sponsors is focusing too much on what they have to sell; instead, the property should emphasize what the sponsor needs to buy to address their problems. This relates to the marketing theory of product-versus-market orientation. People are more successful selling products and sponsorships that consumers are convinced they need, as opposed to products the salesperson is trying to sell. The challenges sponsors face are often associated with identifying and acquiring customers. The stages of buyer readiness referenced in many marketing texts indicate that buyers move through definable stages in the product adoption process (Pride & Ferrell, 2008). You can demonstrate to sponsors precisely how a sponsorship can address these challenges through the scenarios depicted below.

Identification of Product Need

Example: Consumers may realize they have a need for a particular product if they see that product in use in the sport activity or at the event.

Quest for Information

Example: Sponsorships can provide information in the form of brochures, program advertisements, product displays, or public address announcements in order to assist consumers with their quest for increased product knowledge.

Product Evaluation

Example: Consumers may have information about a company's products but may not have actually tried it. Through product sampling, sponsorships can allow consumers to evaluate the product before deciding to purchase it. If a company has a new product, these activities can motivate consumers toward retail purchase.

Purchase of the Product

Example: Many sponsorship packages use coupons as a means to drive sales. These tactics can move in two directions. First, coupons can be made available at the event or, second, sponsors can make discounted ticket coupons available at their retail outlets. Both of these methods have a good history of success. Some success has also been achieved through on-site sales activities.

Customer Satisfaction

Example: Most companies gather data on customer satisfaction. Sporting events can provide an excellent backdrop for these activities. You can set up areas for intensive focus group sessions with an array of customer types. This is an activity many sponsors find desirable.

It must be emphasized that the model does not encourage *crossover* tactics. In other words, you should discuss all of the challenges before proceeding to the solutions segment (known as Phase 3) of the presentation. From a psychological standpoint, this will build momentum for closing the sale. Listening carefully to what the sponsor said during Phase II is critical in presenting the solutions. The following are some concerns frequently expressed by sponsors: "We need to activate our target audience;" "We need a reputable partner;" "Additional media exposure is certainly desirable;" "Can you provide sampling opportunities?" (Stotlar, 2001).

All of these elements were identified as challenges that the NBA could address for Schick Razors through their Official Supplier status. Therefore, the NBA developed extensive product giveaway programs at arenas. In the final analysis it made sense demographically. Schick's target of men 18 to 34 was a perfect match with NBA audiences. Schick also capitalized on their association with the NBA and their target market by sponsoring 700 college tournaments, where the playoffs were conducted at NBA games. Many of Schick's corporate objectives—image enhancement, product trial, and hospitality—tied directly to stages of consumer behavior and were accomplished through their NBA sponsorship.

Closing an agreement and obtaining the payment (known as Phase IV) is typically referred to as "The Ask." Many sport marketers are comfortable making presentations and discussing the virtues of the team or event. However, actually asking someone to hand over a check for $200,000 can be distressing. Negotiating the price of the sponsorship is also a formidable process. As with most business dealings, the physical setting for the negotiation is critical. One approach is to set up a face-to-face meeting, or host it if possible, in order to create an opportunity to demonstrate hospitality. As a side note: Don't pull a Coke out from the refrigerator during your meeting with Pepsi executives.

When the Phoenix Coyotes in NHL scheduled a meeting with Bar S Foods to present sponsorship ideas for the coming season, they proceeded through all of the basic points and then invited the Bar S Foods executives into the front office. There the executives found about 90% of the Coyotes staff having a barbeque lunch, complete with Bar S hotdogs. The Bar S people commented, "Those types of personal touches mean so much, and it has us leaving on such a high note" ("Presenting Sponsor," 2004). Hosting the meeting will also allow you to control the timing more effectively. Occasionally, when you have a meeting scheduled at the sponsor's place of business, key executives may be delayed and end up usurping your time allotment.

During the presentation, avoid using any media that involve turning off the lights. Powerpoint slides should be viewable in room light (try a big-screen TV as opposed to a projector and screen). It is important to watch the reactions of the audience during the presentation. Remember, sometimes a marketer has to spend a bit of money on the presentation to make it effective. The owner of the NBA Denver Nuggets and NHL Colorado Avalanche spent $50,000 on their presentation to Pepsi for title sponsorship of the Pepsi Center in Denver. While the cost was substantial, the presentation was successful.

NEGOTIATIONS

Negotiations must start with an offer, and since you are the one presenting the proposal, making the offer is always your responsibility. If you have done your homework on pricing, the sponsorship should be valued correctly. However, most business executives will issue a counteroffer. First and foremost, you should acknowledge their willingness to work with you as a sponsor. Next, review the benefits and price-value relationship previously presented—this is a strategy that has met with a lot of success. This often has the effect of reinforcing the message and can result in an agreement. If, however, they continue to suggest a price lower than the asking price, you should reduce the sponsorship package and eliminate some of the associated benefits; in essence, offering them a diminished package (Skildum-Reid, 2012). Another option would be to offer to locate a cosponsor to share the costs. At times, it is difficult to walk away from an offer. When the Arizona Diamondbacks in MLB were coming off of a World Series Championship, they made a presentation to a sponsor priced at $1 million, and the sponsor offered $600,000. They had clearly presented more than $1 million in value and had other sponsors involved at that level. As a result, they had to walk away from the deal. One of the primary reasons for rejecting the offer was to protect the integrity of their other partnerships (Brubaker, 2003). Ultimately, if a sponsor remains steadfast with their first offer after you have reviewed the value and offered to find cosponsors, then the meeting should be adjourned as the chances are marginal that an agreement will ever result. If the negotiations are successful and an agreement is reached, then your next step is to establish a timeline for contact finalization.

Industry veteran Ethan Green (2004) provides several useful tips for the negotiating process from the sponsor's standpoint. He suggests that sponsors negotiate an Exit Clause since there are times when situations within the sponsoring company change or the sponsorship fails to deliver on its promised impact. Another clause that should be included is a performance clause. This would tie the sponsorship fee to the claims made by the organization in terms of event attendance, television ratings, or other aspects of the agreement. Such clauses could set a window or conditions under which cancellation would be acceptable or specify the appropriate fees to be reduced. Green also recommends that sponsors consider including exclusive items in the sponsorship package (also noted in Chapter 7). Sport organizations often have access to game-worn jerseys, autographed merchandise, or other unique items that are not readily available to the general public—sponsors could make valuable use of these items with their clients or employees.

MANAGING SPONSOR RELATIONSHIPS

Managing any business relationship is predicated on the contract existing between the two parties. Sponsorship contracts are critical because many of the terms and concepts remain imprecise. Reed (1990) outlined basic rationale for having a contract:

1. Contracts are needed to clarify the rights assigned to the sponsor and specify the rights retained by the sport organization. Problems have sometimes occurred when sponsors attempted to assign some of their rights to another party. Specifically, during one NASCAR racing season, Cingular, a cell phone company, was bought out by AT&T. As a result, AT&T desired to replace the Cingular logo on the racecar with its own logo. NASCAR series title sponsor Sprint, a wireless phone company with category exclusivity obtained after Cingular's deal, challenged the request. Afterward, a thorough review of contract litigation resulted. An out-of-court settlement allowed the use of the AT&T logo on the car through the next season.

2. The contract should clearly define Title Sponsor, Official Supplier, Presenting Sponsor, and other terms used in the relationship. These terms have no universal meaning or legal interpretation other than what is delineated in the contract.

3. A thorough contract will stipulate the size and placement of all event and stadium signage. Detailed descriptions must be included describing the exact location and dimensions of all signage and assigning the responsibility for manufacturing and erecting the signs.

4. Category exclusivity was noted in Chapter 3 as an important benefit. However, the boundaries of sponsor categories are unclear. For instance, does "financial services" cover banks and credit cards? Does it cover investment services? Therefore, considerable attention must be given to setting category parameters.

5. Contracts are also essential in clarifying the attendant liability of all parties involved. In most instances, sponsors will require that the sport entity include them as a coinsurer on all insurance documents. Sponsors will not risk their corporate assets by exposing them through your own failures, crises, or mismanagement.

6. Protecting the event as an intellectual property is another reason for executing a contract. Several years ago, Coors Brewing Company served as Title Sponsor of the Coors Light Silver Bullet Biathlon Series. However, when it came time for renewal after two successful years of the event, Coors delivered a letter to the originators of the event that stated, "While Coors will evaluate your proposal for possible use in the future, it cannot make any commitments until all programs have been reviewed. . . . Please be advised that Coors may be developing similar or

related projects, independent of any promotional ideas, or proposals [XYZ] has submitted" (Stotlar, 1993b, p. 205).

A few weeks later, the organizer received notice that Coors would not be renewing its contract and had, in fact, hired one of the previous organizer's employees to stage an almost identical event for Coors. These types of actions can be reduced through a clause in the contract that restricts the sponsor from staging a similar event for a specified number of years. This is typically called a "covenant not to compete."

7. Contracts are also useful in establishing future rights as a sponsor. Because, in many instances, the full value of sponsorship is often not realized in a single year, many sponsors would like to secure the opportunity to retain their sponsorship status. This is often called the right of first refusal. This clause mandates that you offer future options to continuing sponsors before allowing competitors to sign on. In 2006, an interesting turn of events happened with MasterCard's longtime sponsorship of the FIFA World Cup: Nearing the end of its sponsorship contract, FIFA officials began secret negotiations with MasterCard's rival Visa and announced that they had signed Visa as a new World Cup sponsor. MasterCard immediately sued citing its right of first refusal in the existing contract. The courts ultimately agreed with MasterCard and ordered FIFA to accept the negotiated deal with MasterCard. Within a few days of the ruling, four executives were terminated by FIFA. The right of first refusal does not restrict you from changing prices from year to year, but it does provide the sponsor with the capacity to continue if their objectives are achieved. To extend benefits from sponsor relationships, most sponsors prefer to sign multiyear contracts covering three to five years and to obtain a right of first refusal.

Since sport sponsorship represents a partnership, protecting a sponsor's domain is in the sport marketer's best interest. Attending to these contractual details promotes mutual understanding prior to the implementation of a sponsorship alliance. Hopefully, such a relationship will serve the mutual needs of both parties and provide the desired benefits.

Sponsorship Activation Worksheets

The worksheets guide the development of various sections of a sponsorship plan. The following sheets cover the activation of the sponsorship. Complete this worksheet as you would prepare a sponsorship plan.

Draft a cover letter to the person responsible for sponsorship decisions at the sponsor's headquarters.

_____

_____

_____

_____

_____

_____
_____
_____
_____

Develop an outline for your sponsorship proposal presentation.

_____
_____
_____
_____
_____
_____
_____
_____

Structure your negotiation strategies covering possible challenges from the sponsor.

_____
_____
_____
_____
_____
_____
_____
_____

Delineate all administrative tasks for managing the sponsorship.

_____
_____
_____
_____
_____
_____
_____
_____

9

Managing Sport Sponsorships

INTRODUCTION

The sport organization, as the recipient of the sponsorship dollars, is responsible for demonstrating the value received by the sponsor. First of all, Spoelstra (1997) suggested, "Do whatever it takes to make the sponsorship successful" (p. 173). In his interviews and research with leading sponsors, Stotlar (1999) found several sponsors reported that very few sport organizations followed up their partnership with either final reports or supporting data. The sponsorship manager for a major national banking firm indicated that in her ten years of sponsorship management, only a handful of event managers had submitted reports to her with supporting data. In contrast to this practice, most sponsors now require that fulfillment reports be provided that demonstrate the company's return on the sponsorship investment (Spoelstra, 1997; Stotlar, 1999).

CREATING A SPONSORSHIP REPORT

Almost all sponsorship managers believe that an annual sponsorship report should be delivered to each sponsor detailing the tangible benefits. In its sponsorship contracts, General Motors requires *proof of performance* reports and *fulfillment audits* before final sponsorship payments are made. In this digital age, the Durham Bulls were one of the first organizations to create their fulfillment report on DVD, therein giving sponsors a great opportunity to see, hear, and experience what they got in return for their partnership with the team.

Significant controversy exists surrounding who should be responsible for preparing the report. Many experts suggest that since it was the property that delivered the sponsorship elements, it should have the responsibility to prepare and deliver the fulfillment report. However, others (Seiferheld, 2010; Skildum-Reid, 2012) argue that the property is either incapable or biased in this matter. Seiferheld (2010) notes that "when a property measures sponsorship performance for its partners, it demonstrates good will by assuming the cost and logistics of the research" (p. 20). He also notes that it seems "unfair to expect a property to provide an unbiased assessment regarding the performance of a sponsorship" (p. 20). Skildum-Reid (2012) believes that properties are, however well-intentioned, incapable of conducting the research. She noted "if you are asking the property to measure returns for you, you need to stop it right now. It is unfair to expect that they can measure your results against your objectives" (p. 174). Perhaps one solution is to have both parties develop fulfillment strategies and have a neutral third-party conduct and prepare the analysis (Seiferheld, 2010; Skildum-Reid, 2012). One such example is the International Events Group (IEG), which works as a third-party with both properties and sponsors in defining and measuring objectives. IEG contracted with NASCAR race team Roush-Fenway, and the team's marketing VP commented that prospective sponsors saw the use of a third party as a significantly positive factor (www.sponsorship.com).

For properties that have measured results for their sponsors, these reports typically include samples of all sponsorship materials or photos of sponsor images and signage in a DVD digital scrap book form that graphically conveys the information. Furthermore, the report should relate all of the promotional activities that the team conducted to support the sponsorship. Not only might this make the company liaison feel secure in their sponsorship decision, but it would also provide them with material to justify their actions within the sponsoring corporation.

Skildum-Reid (2012) suggests that sponsors are increasingly demanding a more sophisticated measurement of value. These measures typically parallel those used to evaluate all corporate marketing elements. The measurement problem exists because, while sponsors want to know the exact return on their investment, sponsorship is difficult to measure. We have mistakenly applied standard advertising metrics to sponsorship measurement: While some of the measures are appropriate, others fail to capture the essence of sponsorship value in generating effective results in the minds and hearts of the consumers (Skildum-Reid, 2012).

MEASURING RETURN ON INVESTMENT (ROI)

While many corporate officers use ROI measurements to guide all of their business decisions, the rigidity of this approach may fail to capture the true value of the investment. Sponsorship is not as easily quantified as some other business activities. There are certainly quantitative measures that can be employed, but qualitative measures also have their place.

From a quantitative standpoint, many event managers collect data on awareness and recall of sponsor's signage—for instance, data showing that 50% of fans were able to recognize a sponsor's arena signage. In another study Barros, Barros, Santos, and Chadwick (2007) found recognition rates of up to 70% at the Euro 2004 soccer tournament in Portugal. Pitts's (1998) investigation of sponsor recognition at the Gay Games IV indicated that participants were highly cognizant of sponsor identity. Her findings demonstrated that over 75% of participants were able to correctly name three of the four major sponsors with 57.8% identifying the other. This research protocol has also been applied to the elusive Gen Y population. Bennett, Henson, and Zhang (2002) noted that participants and attendees at action sports events, such as the Gravity Games, were able to recognize the sponsors at an impressive 90% rate. These data would be critically important to sponsors, and it is incumbent for sport managers to collect these types of data and report them to corporate partners.

Skildum-Reid (2012) adamantly refutes this approach. She believes that measuring exposure, event attendance, and logo recognition miss the mark on the value of the sponsorship. While it may be important that the consumers are able to recall the name of the sponsor, it may not affect the purchasing activities or positive consumer behavior. As an example, data from the Winter Olympic Games showed that 72% of people surveyed were able to recognize Visa as an Olympic sponsor. After the Games, 20% of people who recognized Visa as an Olympic sponsor said that they used the credit card company more than the previous month. From its beginning as an Olympic sponsor, Visa's measure of consumer preference as "best overall card" has risen 50%. Their rank as "most accepted card" has doubled. Given that the credit card industry generates over $1 trillion per year in U.S. consumer spending and more than $3 trillion worldwide, these increases in use preference would provide a substantial return on their investment (International Olympic Committee, 2002a; International Olympic Committee, 2002b; "VISA USA," 2004).

Notwithstanding the success of Visa, Stotlar's research (1993) showed that, in general, few people could identify Olympic Sponsors. Most Olympic TOP sponsors had recognition rates of less than 20%. Only two sponsors were able to surpass 50% in consumer recognition as a sponsor. While the data may look dismal, we cannot jump to the conclusion that spectator recognition was the only—or even primary—motivation of the sponsor.

Skildum-Reid (2012) noted that, although sponsor recall has been a popular metric for measuring success, the end result is to influence consumers, not to see if they can remember a sign that may ultimately have little effect on their purchasing decisions. In the case of the Olympics, sponsors reported "hospitality" as a leading objective in providing company executives with an opportunity to interact with their best clients (B2B marketing), yet few of the research studies conducted on the Games address this issue. In any case, additional research would be warranted.

Seaver (2004) noted that a better term and design for assessment is *return on objective* (ROO) as opposed to *return on investment* (ROI). The principle supporting this approach is that a specified value can be placed on attaining a specific objective. Sport marketers could then assess the accomplishment of the objective. For example, in a business-to-business objective to create more favorable opinions about a brand, the sponsor may include hospitality activities at an event. The objective measure, as employed by UPS and their NASCAR sponsorship, would be to track the shipping activities of the attendees against last year's volume (ROI). On the other hand, LG Electronics has been more interested in the perceptions of action sports participants who think that LG is a "cool" brand (ROO). Qualitative interviews with event participants would reveal the answer. The hope of LG is that eventually the "cool" factor would translate to increased sales. In the Best Practice section of this chapter, there is an example of LG's breakout of the ROO from an action sports event where they hope the "cool brand" image will be further enhanced. Similarly, some corporations that sponsor racing hope that the excitement of racing will transfer to their otherwise unexciting product—a task that is difficult to quantify. In experience marketing, companies want to create touch points with their customers. Qualitative research, including interviews and focus groups, are best used to measure these objectives.

Ukman outlined a basic process for collecting and reporting data to sponsors. She identified the first step in the process as setting objectives and baselines: "Articulating measurable objectives is a prerequisite of effective sponsorship measurement" (Ukman, 2004a, p. 3). The objectives should be directional, time-framed, and audience specific. The second step in the process is creating the measurement plan. What types of data are needed to measure the above-stated objectives? Who will be responsible for collecting the data? These issues need to be clarified from the beginning of the sponsorship process. Benchmarks need to be established against which the data can be compared. If a 5% increase in sales is desired, sponsors must know the baseline in order to complete the analysis with post-event data. Data can be collected for multiple sources, such as employees, distributors, spectators, participants, vendors, or the general public. Unfortunately, 86% of sponsors do not spend anything—or spend less than 1%—of their sponsorship budget on measurement. Ukman's third step is implementation of the measurement plan. For example, if the measurement plan was to assess awareness, then data, such as those noted above on recall and recognition, would be collected. However, if the objectives were to evaluate brand loyalty, then data would need to be collected through audience surveys. Questions like, "Would they recommend this brand to friends?" or "How likely would they be to use this brand?" would be appropriate. Finally, the fourth step in the process is to calculate the return on sponsorship. This includes assigning values to the measurement points in the plan.

SPONSOR INTEGRATION

To ensure the success of sponsorship partners, the sport marketer should assist sponsors with fully integrating their sponsorship activities within their company. Of primary concern is the understanding of the sponsorship rationale by company employees—not just the marketing staff but all of the employees. Educating company employees by clarifying the objectives and the resulting benefits can enhance employee support for and involvement in sponsorship activities ("Five Key Factors," 2004). As noted previously, sponsorships are partnerships, and as a result, all facets of implementation, execution, and measurement must be collaborative.

WHY SPONSORS DROP OUT

Sponsors cannot be counted on for an indefinite period as they often drop out for a variety of reasons. Sawyer (1998) identified some of the reasons that sponsors cited for withdrawing from their arrangements. Several sponsors mentioned a decrease in the market value of the event. This was determined either by reduced attendance at a particular event or by a drop in television ratings. When the Women's United Soccer Association (WUSA) folded in 2003, they blamed their demise on lack of sponsorship. The reality was that the WUSA was pricing sponsorship beyond what could be expected in return for value. They were attempting to secure four major sponsors at $10 million each. A review of the opportunities did not show value anywhere near $10 million.

Some proposed that this was due to a bias against females, but a closer look suggests that it was actually due to an overpriced product in a market full of competitors. It also reinforces the notion that the WUSA was more interested in what they had to sell as opposed to what the sponsors might want to buy.

On occasion, the cost of sponsoring an event simply inhibits the company. One illustration of this phenomenon was in tennis with sponsorship of the U.S. Open: "So intertwined was Lipton with the event over the last 13 years that it has become known simply as 'The Lipton'" (Kaplan, 1998a, p. 15). In many ways, the popularity of the event, and tennis in general, priced Lipton out of title sponsorship. Lipton was no longer able to afford title sponsorship of the event, which cost the company $5 million. Furthermore, after eight years of sponsorship with the Open, Pepsi dropped out. A Pepsi executive noted, "The Open is a great hospitality vehicle, but the decision was based on us wanting to concentrate on sports properties that can do more as far as moving cases of soda" (Lefton, 2003, p. 12).

Another regularly cited explanation is a change in corporate direction (Skildum-Reid, 2012). In other words, the company decides that sport sponsorship is no longer in their best interests. One example of this was seen in Kodak's departure as an Olympic sponsor. Kodak's chief business officer said, "We loved the Olympics, but unfortunately, the sponsorship only comes once every two years ("Kodak Refocuses," 2008). Kodak moved into a multiyear partnership with Six Flags theme park. Similarly, Chinese computer manufacturer Lenovo dropped its sponsorship of the Olympics after Beijing 2008 because "the company will focus more on event sponsorship in strategically targeted markets" (Bloom, 2007, p. 3). Interestingly, Taiwanese computer-maker Acer signed up as a replacement only days after Lenovo's announcement not to renew.

Timing and scheduling during any year is an aspect over which the sport manager may have little control. Events and opportunities may come into conflict with other corporate advertising or sponsorship campaigns. This reason alone has left many sport organizers without sponsorship even though their data and proposals were attractive. Sawyer (1998) also found that, while multiple factors and hard data were required to convince a sponsor to initiate a sponsorship, one negative attribute was sufficient to cause a sponsor to drop out.

More recent research has identified several threats to traditional sponsorship success and renewal:

1. Lack of measurement: The inability to track the impact of spending in terms of sales.
2. Clutter: There are way too many other sponsors involved.
3. Cost: Sports are pricing themselves out of the market.
4. Activation: As rights fees rise, there are not as many dollars available for activation.
5. ROI: Properties need to understand that they need to help their partners sell more product instead of focusing on their own business objectives.
6. Category exclusivity: Properties continue to carve up their categories into smaller and less valuable segments. (Spanberg, 2012a, p. 15)

PREVENTING DROPOUT

Ukman (2003b) stated the obvious when she said, "Too many sponsorship programs are dropped, not because they don't have measurable value, but because the value was not measured" (p. 2). Giving service to sponsors can prevent dropout. Simply stated, underserviced (or worse yet, *un*serviced) sponsors leave (Skildum-Reid, 2012). As noted previously, Joyce Julius & Associates has, as its main business, the provision of the type of data that can demonstrate a sponsorship value. Its analysis of sporting event television coverage provides estimates of the advertising value of the corporate logos' appearance, and the announcers' product and corporate mentions in relation to the time of on-screen presence. Supporting information should also be collected and provided by the sport organization. Factors such as attendance and crowd demographics are of particular importance to sponsors and are almost always readily available. Additional information on the psychographics, buying habits, attitudes, and loyalty of attendees is also critical for sponsors. The more you know about your event and its audience, the more power you will have in attracting and keeping sponsors.

SUMMARY

As has been suggested, data needed to justify involvement in sport sponsorships are important to both the event owner and the sponsor. The best practice is to complete an accurate and extensive post-event report that details the value of the sponsorship. As a final note, if you don't provide this information, the company executive who signed the $300,000 sponsorship check may not still be employed when renewal comes around. And they certainly won't be happy with a cancelled check as the only feedback on their investment. Hopefully, by following the guidelines and recommendations presented throughout this workbook, you will be successful in developing and implementing successful sport sponsorship plans of your own.

Best Practice LG Action Sports Championships

LG Electronics, a large Korean-based company known mostly for its cell phones, and also a producer of digital appliances and flat screen televisions, was title sponsor of the 2003 LG Action Sports Championships held in Los Angeles. Below you will find information ranging from their objectives to the post-event measurement activities. The key points in this case include LG's integration, activation, and measurement practices.

LG Objectives
1. To increase brand awareness and create familiarity between LG and the target audience in action sports and music through pre-event marketing initiatives and on-site activation.

2. To build a compelling interactive experience in order to engage the target audience in a personal and memorable way so that LG's sponsorship will remain with the consumer long after the event is over.

Event Data

Attendance: 31,368 attendees, 45% of which fall into the 15 to 17 age group. 73% of attendees had a cell phone and the remainder had a high intent to purchase.

Sales Potential

Potential LG cell phone purchases: 25% of attendees, or roughly 8,000 people, will purchase cell phones in the next year. The average price of a phone is $200. 2,640 were either likely or somewhat likely, when phones were discounted 50%, to purchase LG. Therefore, the market sales potential is $528,000.

Key Marketing Elements

Pre-Event Television

Seventy-five 30-second placements generating 1.2 million impressions valued at $303,400.

Road to the LG Action Sports Championships featuring 399,000 60-minute placements valued at $72,000.

Pre-Event Online

LG "Pic Trick" voting at website, and randomly drawn product giveaways. 3,796 voters from 4,662 unique visitors valued at $8,400.

On-site Activation

LG lounge . . . VIP hospitality . . . Music stage . . . LG phone girls . . . Pic Trick sweepstakes . . . Enter to win raffle . . . Athlete appearances . . . Product demonstration kiosks . . . "Name That Tone" game . . . LG cell phone inflateables . . . Participant gift packs with LG products and logo souvenirs

Management Worksheets

The worksheets guide the development of various sections of a sponsorship plan. The following sheets cover the management of the sponsorship including the final report to the sponsor. Complete this worksheet as you would prepare a sponsorship plan.

Identify the person responsible for sponsor services.

_____

_____

_____

_____

_____

_____

_____

_____

_____

Complete the post-event report

List the event date: _____

Report the attendance: _____

Calculate the audience (immediate and mediated numbers):

_____

_____

_____

_____

_____

_____

_____

_____

Report the demographic/psychographic profile of the audience.

_____

_____

_____

_____

_____

_____

_____

_____

Specify the media coverage and compute the commercial value
attained.

_____

_____

_____

_____

_____

_____

_____

Record the impressions/recognition data for all sponsorship elements.

_____
_____
_____
_____
_____
_____
_____
_____
_____

Record the qualitative data for appropriate sponsorship elements.

_____
_____
_____
_____
_____
_____
_____
_____
_____

Prepare the final report for the sponsor (as applicable).

_____
_____
_____
_____
_____
_____
_____
_____

References

2013 sponsorship outlook: Spending increase is double-edged sword. (2013, January 7). *IEG Sponsorship Report*. Retrieved from http://www .sponsorship.com/iegsr/2013/01/07/2013-Sponsorship-Outlook—Spending-Increase-Is-Dou.aspx

A tale of two districts: Texas schools take a different approach to sponsorship. (2003). Retrieved from http://www.sponsorship.com

Allen, S. (1998). *Pitching with a pen*. Holmdel, NJ: Allen Consulting, Inc.

Amis, J., Pant, N., & Slack, T. (1997). Achieving a sustainable competitive advantage: A resource-based view of sport sponsorship. *Journal of Sport Management, 11*(1), 80–95.

Amshay, T., & Brian, V. (1998, July 20–26). Sport sponsorship sword cuts both ways. *SportsBusiness Journal*, 23.

Barros, C. P., Barros, C., Santos, A., & Chadwick, S. (2007). Sponsorship brand recall at the Euro 2004 soccer tournament. *Sport Marketing Quarterly, 16*(3), 161–170.

Baseball's Cubs run free funeral promotion. (2004). *Stadia*. Retrieved from http://www.stadia.tv.archive/user/news_article.tpl?id=20040521160041

Bayor, L. (1996, May 20). Atlanta fends off megasigns. *Advertising Age*, 30.

Bennett, G., Henson, R., & Zhang, J. (2002). Action sports sponsorship recognition. *Sport Marketing Quarterly, 11*(3), 25–34.

Big South. (2010, May 24). *Big South Conference*. Retrieved from www.bigsouthsports.com//ViewArticle.dbml?DB_OEM_ID=4800&ATCLID=204950349

Bloom, H. (2007, December 5). That was quick, Lenovo out as Olympic Sponsor. *Sport Business Network Daily Dose*, 3.

Boland, R. (2010). Brady's under armour deal to include equity stake—why don't more? *Forbes*. Retrieved from http://www.forbes.com/sites/sportsmoney/2010/11/08/bradys-under-armour-deal-to-include-equity-stake-why-dont-more/

Boyd, T., & Shank, M. (2004). Athletes as product endorsers: The effect of gender and product relatedness. *Sport Marketing Quarterly, 13*(2), 82–93.

Broncos announce partnership with Buick. (2012, July 26). *The Denver Post*. Retrieved from www.denverpost.com/breakingnews/ci_21166608/broncos-announce-partnership-buick

Brooks, C. M. (2001, Spring). Using sex appeal as a sport promotion strategy. *Women in Sport & Physical Activity Journal, 10*(1), 1–11.

Brooks, C. M., & Harris, K. K. (1998). Celebrity athlete endorsement: An overview of the key theoretical issues. *Sport Marketing Quarterly, 7*(2), 34–44.

Brubaker, S. (2003). Negotiations part one: Executives outline approach to say no to a prospective sponsor. *Team Marketing Report, 15*(4), 7.

Burton, R., & O'Reilly, N. (2010, September 27–October 3). Could sponsor alliances spread to North American sports? *SportsBusiness Journal*, 21.

Carey, J. (2012, March 15). More high schools playing the sponsorship game. *USA Today*, 16C.

Carter, L., & Wilkinson, I. (2002, July). *Reasons for sponsoring the Sydney 2000 Olympic Games*. Paper presented at ANZMAC 2000 Visionary Marketing for the 21st Century: Facing the Challenge.

Copeland, R., Frisby, W., & McCarville, R. (1996). Understanding the sport sponsorship from a corporate perspective. *Journal of Sport Management, 10*(1), 32–48.

Cordiner, R. (2002, January). Sponsors of the wide world of sport—what's in it for them? *Sports Marketing*, 14–16.

Cordova, J. (1996, January). *Coca-Cola's sponsorship objectives*. Paper presented at the National Sports Forum, Colorado Springs, CO.

Currie, N. (2004, March). Interview with Nigel Currie, joint chairman European Sponsorship Association. *International Journal of Sports Marketing and Sponsorship*, 246–251.

Cutler, M. (2012, November 14). London 2012 Olympics revenue breakdown revealed. *Sport Business*. Retrieved from www.sportbusiness.com/news/186649/london-2012-olympics-revenue-breakdown-revealed

Dannon sponsorship stirs 3-to-1 return. (2003). *IEG Sponsorship Report, 22*(21), 1–2.

Danylchuk, K. (1998, November). *Sponsorship of the LPGA du Maurier Classic: Will it go up in smoke?* Paper presented at the Conference of the Sport Management Association of Australia and New Zealand, Gold Coast, Australia.

Drayer, J., Shapiro, S., & Morse, A. (2012). Dynamic ticket pricing in sport: A conceptual model. 2012 Sport marketing Association Annual Conference, Orlando, FL.

EA Sports gives teams and sponsors numerous options for video games. (1998, March). *Team Marketing Report*, 6.

Eaton, B. (2004, May 19). *VISA USA strengthens ties with USA Gymnastics through 2008.* Retrieved from http://www.sponsorship.com

Endorsement comings and goings. (2010, September 20–26). *SportsBusiness Journal*, 32.

Evinrude renews long-term sponsorship of FLW Outdoors. (2004). Retrieved from http://www.sponsorship.com

FDA. (2012). Overview of the Family Smoking Prevention and Tobacco Control Act: Consumer fact sheet. *U.S. Food and Drug Administration.* Retrieved from http://www.fda.gov/tobaccoproducts/guidancecomplianceregulatoryinformation/ucm246129.htm#

Financial. (n.d.). *Team USA.* Retrieved from http://www.teamusa.org/About-the%20USOC/Organization/Financial.aspx

Fink, J., Kensicki, L., Fitzgerald, M., & Brett, M. (2004, June). *Using female athletes as endorsers of events: Attractiveness versus expertise.* Paper presented at the Conference of the North American Society for Sport Management, Atlanta, GA.

Finley, B. (1998, December 24). Utah bid probed by feds. *Denver Post*, pp. 1A, 15A.

Five key factors that ensure relevant activation and sponsorship success. (2004). *IEG Sponsorship Report*, 23(11), 1–3.

Freedman, J. (n.d.). The 50 highest-earning American athletes. *SI.com.* Retrieved from http://sportsillustrated.cnn.com/specials/fortunate50-2011/index.html

Freedman, J. (2008). Ranking the 50 highest-earning athletes in the U.S. Retrieved from http://sportsillustrated.cnn.com/more/specials/fortunate50/2008/index.html

Freidman, A. (1999, March-April 4). Rare glimpse at the selling of a stadium. *SportsBusiness Journal*, 36–37.

Gatlin, G. (2003, December 31). In endorsements, youth wins. *Boston Herald*, p. O27.

Giannoulakis, C., Stotlar, D. K., & Chatziefstathiou, D. (2008). Olympic sponsorship: Evolution, challenges and impact on the Olympic movement. *International Journal of Sport Management and Sponsorship*, 9, 256–270.

Goldberg, R. (1998a, June 22–28). Co-branding ideal for sponsors who want to go the extra mile. *SportsBusiness Journal*, 22.

Goldberg, R. (1998b, June 22–28). Toughest task: Measuring results. *SportsBusiness Journal*, 29.

Goldman, L. (2000). Going to xtremes. *Forbes*, 165(8), 18.

Graham, S. (1998, June 22–28). Rights deals making a play for sales value. *SportsBusiness Journal*, 34.

Greater TOP support. (1999, January). *Olympic Marketing Matters*, 10.

Green, E. (2004). Ethan Green's ten tips of improve sponsor negotiations. Retrieved from http://www.migalareport.com

Greenwald, L., & Fernandez-Balboa, J. M. (1998). Trends in the sport marketing industry and in the demographics of the United States: Their effect on the strategic role of grassroots sport sponsorship in corporate America. *Sport Marketing Quarterly*, 7(4), 35–48.

Grey, A. M., & Skildum-Reid, K. (2007). *Sponsorship seekers toolkit* (2nd ed.). Sydney, Australia: McGraw Hill.

Hagstrom, R. (1998). *The NASCAR way.* New York, NY: Wiley.

Hein, K. (2003, July 14). A broken field of dreams. *Brandweek*, 15.

Highest-paid athletes 2012—world's richest athletes. (2012, June 19). *The Richest.* Retrieved from www.therichest.org/sports/forbes-highest-paid-athletes/

HopeLine success stories. (n.d.). *Verizon Wireless.* Retrieved from aboutus.verizonwireless.com/communityservice/PhoneDrives.html

Hotzau, A. (2007, April). Ambush marketing. *Sport Decision Intelligence Report*, 1–3.

Hugo Boss renews Davis Cup tie through 2012. (2007). (n.d.). Retrieved from www.sponsorship.com/news-information/news/pre-kentico-archives

IEG property survey reveals deepening sponsor pools. (2011, December 5). *IEG Sponsorship Report.* Retrieved from http://www.sponsorship.com/IEGSR/2011/12/05/IEG-Property-Survey-Reveals-Deepening-Sponsor-Pool.aspx

IEG. (n.d.). Retrieved from http://www.sponsorship.com/Resources/Sponsorship-Spending.aspx

IEG survey: Cold calls rule. (2007, October 15). *IEG Sponsorship Report*, 26(19), 1, 4–5.

International Olympic Committee. (2002a). *Olympic marketing fact file.* Lausanne, Switzerland: International Olympic Committee.

International Olympic Committee. (2002b). *Salt

Lake 2002 marketing report. Lausanne, Switzerland: International Olympic Committee.

International Olympic Committee. (2004). *Olympic marketing fact file.* Lausanne, Switzerland: International Olympic Committee.

International Olympic Committee. (2012). *Olympic marketing fact file.* Retrieved from www.olympic.org/Documents/IOC_Marketing/OLYMPIC-MARKETING-FACT-FILE-2012.pdf

Irwin, R. L., & Sutton, W. A. (1994). Sport sponsorship objectives: An analysis of their relative importance for major corporate sponsors. *European Journal of Sport Management, 1*(2), 93–101.

Irwin, R. L., Assimakopoulos, M. K., & Sutton, W. A. (1994). A model for screening sport sponsorship opportunities. *Journal of Promotion Management, 2*(3/4), 53–69.

Irwin, R., Lackowitz, T., Cornwell, B., & Clark, J. (2003). Cause-related sport sponsorship: An assessment of spectator beliefs, attitudes and behavioral intentions. *Sport Marketing Quarterly, 12*(3), 131–137.

Isidore, C. (2004). *Big win for the little guys.* Retrieved from http://www.money.cnn.com

It's official—London 2012 to be biggest Paralympic Games ever. (2012, May 21). Retrieved from http://www.paralympic.org/news/it-s-official-london-2012-be-biggest-paralympic-games-ever

Jones, I. (2012, August 6). An Olympic-sized income gap even among our world class athletes. *Colorlines.com.* Retrieved from colorlines.com/archives/2012/08/uss_olympic-sized_income_gap_exists_even_among_our_world_class_athletes.html

Jones, P. D. (1997, January). Better to give and to receive. *Hemispheres,* 33–38.

Joyce Julius & Associates. (2008). *Second look.* Retrieved March 8, 2008, from http://www.joycejulius.com/newletter/a-second-lookmar-2008.htm

Joyce, M. (2003, June 23–29). Alt-sport execs see growth and growing pains for category's events and sponsors. *SportsBusiness Journal,* 8.

Kaplan, D. (1998a, September 7–13). Lipton to bow out of title sponsorship. *SportsBusiness Journal,* 15.

Kaplan, D. (1998b, September 7–13). Venus patches rift with WTA. *SportsBusiness Journal,* 9.

Kaplan, D. (2007, October 8–14). Upshaw: Apparel fines from NFL 'out of hand.' *SportsBusiness Journal, 10*(19), 5.

Kaplan, D. (2008, June 16–22). EA's contract with NFLPA. *SportsBusiness Journal, 11*(9), 4.

Kaplan, D. (2012, August 27–September 2). Cowboys sell experiences on Living Social. *SportsBusiness Journal,* 3.

Keeping the Olympics' ideal. (1997, April). *Sport Business,* 32–33.

Keppler, J. (2013, January 27). Kelly Clark takes Snowboard Superpipe gold at X Games Aspen. *The Ski Channel.* Retrieved from http://www.theskichannel.com/news/20130127/kelly-clark-takes-snowboard-superpipe-gold-at-x-games-aspen/

Kodak refocuses, repurposes role of sponsorship. (2008). Retrieved from http://www.sponsorship.com

Kuzma, J. R., Shanklin, W. L., & McCally, J. F. (1993). Number one principle for sporting events seeking corporate sponsors: Meet benefactor's objectives. *Sport Marketing Quarterly, 2*(3), 27–32.

Lauletta, S. (2003). Negotiations part one: Executives outline approach to say no to a prospective sponsor. *Team Marketing Report, 15*(4), 8.

Lefton, T. (2003, October 6–12). Pepsi out as sponsor of US Open tennis. *SportsBusiness Journal,* 12.

Lefton, T. (2012a). Taking the Subway. *SportsBusiness Journal, 15*(30), 12.

Lefton, T. (2012b, December 3–9). A-B makes Bud Light the key to unlocking in-venue content. *SportsBusiness Journal,* 16.

Lindsay, E. (2008, January 14–20). A futile search. *SportsBusiness Journal, 10*(37), 24.

Lombardo, J. (2004, July 19–25). Nike endorsers will dominate Reebok-clad US hoops team. *SportsBusiness Journal,* 5.

Long, D. (2012, July 11). U.S. Army to discontinue NASCAR sponsorship in 2013. *USA Today.* Retrieved from usatoday30.usatoday.com/sports/motor/nascar/story/2012-07-10/Army-wont-return-to-NASCAR-in-2013/56126666/1

Macnow, G. (1989, September). Sports tie-ins help firms score big. *IEG Sponsorship Report,* 1.

Marsano, W. (1987, September). A five ring circus. *Northwest,* 64–69.

McCarthy, M. (2003, August 22). Win or lose, drawing endorsements is key. *USA Today,* p. 1B.

McCarville, R., & Copeland, B. (1994). Understanding sport sponsorship through exchange theory. *Journal of Sport Management, 8*(2), 102–114.

McDonald, M. (1998, June). *Sport sponsorship and the role of personality matching.* Paper presented at the Conference of the North American Society for Sport Management, Buffalo, NY.

McKelvey, M. (2003, Winter). Commercial branding: The final frontier or false start for athletes' use of temporary tattoos as body billboards. *Journal of the Legal Aspects of Sport, 6*(4). Retrieved from LexisNexis database.

Michel, A. (1991, October). *Economics of the 1992 Albertville Olympics*. Paper presented at the International Sport Business Conference, Columbia, SC.

Mickle, T. (2008a, January 23–February 3). Translating into an endorsement. *SportsBusiness Journal, 10*(39), 1.

Mickle, T. (2008b, June 16–22). USOC tries to cap swimming deals. *SportsBusiness Journal, 11*(9), 1, 6.

Mickle, T. (2011, January 3–9). Action athletes gaining mainstream appeal. *SportsBusiness Journal*, 5.

Migala, D. (2003). Turning cold calls into hot leads. *Migala Report*. Retrieved from http://www.migalareport.com

Migala, D. (2004). What's the buzz: Activation is the buzzword among marketers. *Migala Report*. Retrieved from http://www.migalareport.com

Migala, D. (2007a). Attention: How to get noticed by a sponsor in a modern sponsorship sales environment. *Migala Report*. Retrieved from http://www.migalareport.com

Migala, D. (2007b). Key to new sponsor revenues. *Migala Report*. Retrieved from http://www.migalareport.com

Motion, J., Leitch, S., & Brodie, R. (2003). Equity in corporate cobranding. *European Journal of Marketing, 37*(7/8), 1080–1094.

Muellner, A. (1998, August 3–9). Nike ups its investment in Miami community causes. *SportsBusiness Journal*, 8.

Mullen, L., & Smith, M. (2012, May 21–27). Change may affect future pros' equipment deals. *SportsBusiness Journal*, 9.

Mullen, L. (2012, August 13–19). Teams try to link sponsors, athletes. *SportsBusiness Journal*, 8.

Murray, C. (2012, July). Olympic Games set to break $8bn revenues barrier in four-year cycle ending with London 2012. *Sportcal*. Retrieved from www.sportcal.com/pdf/gsi/Sportcal_Issue 26_6-9.pdf

Mushett, M. (1995, June). *Sponsorship and the Paralympic Games*. Paper presented at the Conference of the North American Society for Sport Management, Atlanta, GA.

Myerson, A. R. (1996, May 31). Olympic sponsors battling to defend turf. *New York Times*, pp. D1, D17.

Nautica signs apparel sponsorship with US sailing teams. (2004, May 21). Retrieved from http://www.sponsorship.com

NCAA. (n.d.). The NCAA's advertising and promotional standards. *The National Collegiate Athletic Association*. Retrieved from http://www.ncaa.org/wps/wcm/connect/broadcast/media/broadcasting/broadcasting+manual/sect3/advstand

Odell, P. (2012). Tune up your experiential marketing for 2012. *Promo*. Retrieved from http://www.chiefmarketer.com/event-marketing/tune-your-experiential-marketing-2012

Olympic Fact File. (1998). Lausanne, Switzerland: International Olympic Committee.

Olympic Games media kit. (n.d.). *Visa*. Retrieved from http://corporate.visa.com/newsroom/media-kits/olympic.shtml#logos

Olympic sponsorship 'changed our mindset' claims Proctor & Gamble director. (2012, October 1). *SportsBusiness Daily Global*. Retrieved from http://www.sportsbusinessdaily.com/Global/Issues/2012/10/01/Marketing-and-Sponsorship/ProctorGamble.aspx

Pepsi wants bigger number of smaller multicultural properties. (2004, May 3). *IEG Sponsorship Report, 23*(8), 1–3.

Performance Research. (2004). *Sponsorship spending and decision making*. Retrieved from http://www.performanceresearch.com/sponsorship-spending.htm

Pitts, B. G. (1998). An analysis of sponsorship recall during Gay Games IV. *Sport Marketing Quarterly, 7*(4), 11–18.

Pitts, B. G., & Stotlar, D. K. (2013). *Fundamentals of Sport Marketing* (4th ed.). Morgantown, WV: Fitness Information Technology.

Ponturo, T. (2002). *What sponsors want*. Panel discussion at the 2002 National Sports Forum, Pittsburgh, PA.

Poole, M. (2003, October 27–November 2). It's a new sponsorship world and agencies can thrive if they adapt. *SportsBusiness Journal*, 14.

Popke, M. (2002, October). Your name here. *Athletic Business*, 42–44.

Pride, W. M., & Ferrell, O. C. (2008). *Marketing* (14th ed.). New York, NY: Houghton Mifflin Company.

Product integration: Not just for technology companies anymore. (2004, May 3). Assertions. *IEG Sponsorship Report, 23*(8), 1, 3.

PwC outlook for the global sports market to 2015. (n.d.). *PricewaterhouseCoopers*. Retrieved from http://www.pwc.com/sportsoutlook

Race fans continue to 'embrace engagement. (2012, November 26). *Sportsbusiness Journal*. Retrieved from http://www.sportsbusinessdaily.com/Journal/Issues/2012/11/26/Research-and-Ratings/NASCAR-Sponsor-Loyalty.aspx

Reed, M. H. (1990). *Legal aspects of promoting and sponsoring events.* Chicago, IL: International Events Group.

Reynolds, M. (1998, June 22–28). Women's sport: A growth area. *SportsBusiness Journal*, 30.

Rick Hendrick, owner. (n.d.). *Hendrick Motorsports.* Retrieved from www.hendrickmotorsports.com /about/rick

Ries, A., & Trout, J. (1986). *Positioning: The battle for your mind.* New York, NY: McGraw-Hill.

Rovell, D. (2004). *Sports biz.* Retrieved from http:// sports.espn.go.com

Roy, D., & Graeff, T. (2003). Consumer attitudes toward cause-related marketing activities in professional sport. *Sport Marketing Quarterly*, *12*(3), 163–172.

Rozin, S. (1998, February 21). Why corporate support is good business. *Forbes Special Advertising Section*, 42–48.

Sawyer, L. (1998, January). *Why sponsors drop out.* Paper presented at the National Sports Forum, Boston, MA.

SDGLN Staff. (2010, July 20). America's gay buying power projected at $743 billion in 2010. *San Diego Gay & Lesbian News.* Retrieved from sdgln.com/news/2010/07/20/america-s-gay-buying-power-projected-743-billion-2010

Seaver, R. (1996, January). *Survey of the industry.* San Diego, CA: Seaver Marketing Group.

Seaver, R. (2004). *2004 corporate sponsorship survey report.* San Diego, CA: Seaver Marketing Group.

Seiferheld, S. (2010, July 26–August 1). Is measurement up to properties or sponsors? *SportsBusiness Journal*, 20.

Seiferheld, S. (2011, October 3–9). To get the most out of a partnership, brands must AIM high. *SportsBusiness Journal*, 15.

Shaun White shares no. 1 in Forbes' winter Olympian Earnings list. (2010, February 12). *SportsBusiness Daily.* Retrieved from www.sportsbusinessdaily.com/Daily/Issues/2010/02/Issue-105 /Olympics/Shaun-White-Shares-No-1-In-Forbes -Winter-Olympian-Earnings-List.aspx

Skildum-Reid, K. (2007). *Ambush marketing toolkit.* Sydney, Australia: McGraw-Hill.

Skildum-Reid, K. (2008a). *All our funds are currently committed.* Retrieved from http://www .powersponsorship.com/blog.aspx#136

Skildum-Reid, K. (2008b). *It's all about you.* Retrieved from http://www.powersponsorship.com /blog.aspx#136

Skildum-Reid, K. (2008c). *Image transfer.* Retrieved from http://www.powersponsorship.com/blog .aspx#136

Skildum-Reid, K. (2012). The corporate sponsorship toolkit. Sydney, Australia: Freya Press.

Smart brand vehicles to lead runners in the 108th Boston Marathon. (2004). Retrieved from http:// www.sponsorship.com

Smith, M. (2012, April 30–May 6). Masters sells out new hospitality area. *SportsBusiness Journal*, 3.

Spanberg, E. (2011, October 3–9). Leagues script options for TV movie exposure. *SportsBusiness Journal*, 22.

Spanberg, E. (2012a, March 26–April 1). The challenge: Stand out amid the clutter. *SportsBusiness Journal*, 15.

Spanberg, E. (2012b, March 26–April 1). Employee benefits. *SportsBusiness Journal*, 13.

Spoelstra, J. (1997). *Ice to the Eskimos.* New York, NY: Harper Business.

Sponsors identify peak-performing properties. (2008, July 14). *IEG Sponsorship Report*, *27*(13), 1, 3–4.

"The Sponsorship Effect" gathered over 250 industry professionals to network and brainstorm. (2011, November 14). Retrieved from http://www.think sponsorship.com/Pages/content/Index.asp?Page ID=186

Sportvision. (n.d.). In-studio broadcast services: Sports. Retrieved from http://www.sportvision .com/sports

Staying ahead of the Games: Visa banks and merchants post Olympic results. (2004). *IEG Sponsorship Report*, *23*(14), 7.

Stone, G., Joseph, M., & Jones, M. (2003). An exploratory study on the use of sport celebrities in advertising: A content analysis. *Sport Marketing Quarterly*, *12*(2), 94–102.

Stotlar, D. K. (1993a). Sponsorship and the Olympic winter games. *Sport Marketing Quarterly*, *2*(3), 35–46.

Stotlar, D. K. (1993b). *Successful sport marketing.* Dubuque, IA: Brown & Benchmark.

Stotlar, D. K. (1997, June). *Xerox: A case study of Olympic sponsorship.* Paper presented at the Annual Conference of the North American Society for Sport Management, San Antonio, TX.

Stotlar, D. K. (1999). Sponsorship in North America: A survey of sport executives. *Journal of Sport Marketing and Sponsorship*, *1*(1), 87–100.

Stotlar, D. K. (2001). *Developing successful sport marketing plans.* Morgantown, WV: Fitness Information Technology.

Strategic philanthropy: Building social capital and financial returns. (2004). Retrieved from http:// www.sponsorship.com/sproducts/109_product _agenda.asp

Summary of NFL player benefits. (n.d.). Retrieved from http://www.delducasports.com/assets/files/Summary-of-NFL-Player-Benefits.pdf

Talalay, S. (2008, February 12). New website connects Florida Panthers' business partners. *Florida Sun Sentinel*, p. B1.

Thwaites, D., & Aguilar-Manjarrez, R. (1997). *Sport sponsorship development among leading Canadian companies*. Montpellier, France: Forth European Congress on Sport Management.

TOP IV Programme. (1997, Summer). *Olympic Marketing Matters*, 8.

Two new partners. (1997, Summer). *Olympic Marketing Matters*, 9.

Ukman, L. (1995a). *IEG's complete guide to sponsorship*. Chicago, IL: International Events Group.

Ukman, L. (1995b, December 4). Back to basics. *IEG Sponsorship Report*, *14*(24), 2.

Ukman, L. (1997a, January 17). Assertions. *International Events Group*. Retrieved from http://www.sponsorship.com

Ukman, L. (1997b, August 18). Assertions. *IEG Sponsorship Report*, *18*(19), 2.

Ukman, L. (1998a, March 20). Assertions. *IEG Sport Sponsorship Report*, *19*(5), 2.

Ukman, L. (1998b, October 26). Assertions. *IEG Sponsorship Report*, *19*(20), 2.

Ukman, L. (2003a). Assertions. *IEG Sponsorship Report*, *22*(21), 2.

Ukman, L. (2003b). Assertions. *IEG Sponsorship Report*, *22*(24), 2.

Ukman, L. (2004a). *Return on sponsorship*. Chicago, IL: International Events Group.

Ukman, L. (2004b, May 3). Assertions. *IEG Sponsorship Report*, *23*(8), 1–3.

Ukman, L. (2004c, May 31). Assertions. *IEG Sponsorship Report*, *23*(10), 2.

Ukman, L. (2008, March 17). Decision maker survey shows confidence in sponsorship. *Sponsorship Report*, *27*(5), 1–3.

University of Nebraska Board of Regents. (n.d.). Retrieved from http://www.sports-city.org/index.php

U.S. Paralympics. (n.d.). Retrieved from http://www.teamusa.org/US-Paralympics/Resources/US-Olympian-and-Paralympian-Association.aspx

Veltri, F. (1996). *Recognition of athlete-endorsed products*. Paper presented at the Conference of the North American Society for Sport Management, Frederickton, NB.

Visa USA making the most of 2004 Olympic Games with marketing campaign. (2004, March 31) [Press release]. San Francisco, CA: Visa USA.

Wall-Doe. (2012, September 3). Inside the American Express fan experience at the U.S. Open 2012. *The Source*. Retrieved from www.thesource.com/articles/242428/Inside-the-American-Express-Fan-Experience-at-the-US-Open-2012/274/Source-Sports?thesource-prod=pnuq95ikk66q9d24qc88jfhk83

Wells, J. (1996, June 10). The big money man. *Macleans*, 52–56.

Wilkinson, D. G. (1986). *Sport Marketing Institute*. Willowdale, Ontario: Sport Marketing Institute.

Williamson, E. (2004). Gulf States Toyota. *Migala Report*. Retrieved from http://www.migalareport.com

Index

About the Author

David K. Stotlar, EdD

Dr. David K. Stotlar teaches on the University of Northern Colorado faculty in the areas of sport marketing, sponsorship, and event management. He also serves as Director of the School of Kinesiology & Physical Education at the same institution. Dr. Stotlar has had more than 60 articles published in professional journals and has written several textbooks and book chapters in sport management and marketing. He has made numerous presentations at international and national professional conferences. On several occasions, he has served as a consultant in sport management to various sport professionals; and in the area of sport marketing and sponsorship, to multinational corporations and international sport managers.

Dr. Stotlar was selected by the United States Olympic Committee as a delegate to the International Olympic Academy in Greece and the World University Games Forum in Italy and served as a venue media center supervisor for the 2002 Olympic Games. He has conducted international seminars in sport management and marketing for the Hong Kong Olympic Committee, the National Sports Council of Malaysia, Mauritius National Sports Council, the National Sports Council of Zimbabwe, the Singapore Sports Council, the Chinese Taipei University Sport Federation, the Bahrain Sport Institute, the government of Saudi Arabia, the South African National Sports Congress, and the Association of Sport Sciences in South Africa. Dr. Stotlar's contribution to the profession includes an appointment as Coordinator of the Sport Management Program Review Council (NASPE/NASSM) from 1999–2001. He previously served as Chair of the Council on Facilities and Equipment of the American Alliance for Health, Physical Education, Recreation and Dance, and as a board member and later as President of the North American Society for Sport Management. Dr. Stotlar was a member of the initial group of professionals inducted as NASSM Research Fellows. He is also a founding member of the Sport Marketing Association.